Improve Your Communication

THE SUNDAY TIMES

Improve Your Communication Skills

Alan Barker

△ KOGAN PAGE | *CREATING SUCCESS*

First published in 2000

Kogan Page Limited
120 Pentonville Road
London N1 9JN

British Library Cataloguing in Publication Data

A CIP record for this book is available from the British Library.

ISBN 0 7494 3262 4

Typeset by Jean Cussons Typesetting, Diss, Norfolk
Printed and bound in Great Britain by Clays Ltd, St Ives plc

contents

about this book

If you're not communicating, you're not managing.

Most people can communicate very well. But you may not recognise the skills that you use. And that means you could find it hard to develop these skills or to transfer them from one situation to another. You may have no problem holding conversations in the staff restaurant, the gym or the pub. Carrying those skills into interviews, presentations, reports and meetings is another matter.

What *is* communication? Many people think that it's about giving information. It's not. Communication is about communing. Scientists think that language – or rather, the languages of speech, body movement, gesture – grew initially out of grooming. Chimps and other primates groom each other to establish and maintain relationships within the group. As groups became larger, and group relationships became more complicated, there simply wasn't enough time to do all the grooming that was necessary. So a form of shorthand was invented: language. Chimps pick fleas off each other; humans hold conversations.

This view of communication helps understanding of why it so often goes wrong. You can't communicate once and imagine that the job is done. Communication, like grooming, is a continuous activity; we need to do it continuously. Conversations at work are never merely about facts and figures; they always include the relationship.

There is a difference between humans and the other primates, of course. People communicate, not only to groom, but also to persuade. And the currency of persuasion is ideas. It's ideas that make things happen. You can't do your work effectively unless you can express your ideas and persuade others to listen to them. You'll do your work even better if you can encourage others to give you their ideas.

This book will help you communicate to get results. It will help you express your ideas and enquire into the ideas of others. It begins with conversation, and extends step by step through the more complex varieties of conversation that you will engage in at work: interviews, presentations and written documents.

Throughout, I've used models to help increase your under-standing. Models simplify reality; good models simplify help-fully. In the thick of it, when life gets complicated, when people act unpredictably and when conversations get heated, models help people see more clearly and act more rationally. The models in this book help me; I hope they will help you.

I'd like you to think of this book as a gateway to other ways of learning and developing your skills. At the very end, I offer some suggestions for further development.

the process of communication

'Let's face it, it all comes down to communication.' How many times have you heard – or spoken – those words as you catalogue the woes that afflict your organisation?

The ability to communicate clearly has never been more important. Working patterns are becoming more flexible and less predictable. The command and control structures of our parents' generation have given way to matrix management and networking, to outsourcing and partnership, to knowledge management and business intelligence. Managers now need to communicate effectively with a far wider range of people than before. And more quickly, too: today's market information is in the recycling bin tomorrow.

And yet, communication remains a major problem in organisations. In survey after survey, managers have rated failures in communication as the most important problem in their companies.

Communication can, of course, still be remarkably effective. The MD's efforts to communicate the latest corporate change programme may fall at the first hurdle; but rumours of imminent job losses can spread like wildfire. If only formal communication could achieve half the success of gossip and chat!

what is communication?

I often ask this question at the start of training programmes and seminars. After a little thought, most people come up with a definition that is about transmitting and receiving information. A little more thought might produce the word *exchange*. This is more satisfactory, but it still assumes that communication is about moving something: about conveying, or sending, or delivering, some commodity called 'information'.

In fact, the word has quite a different root meaning. It derives from the Latin *communis*, meaning 'common', or 'shared'. It belongs to the family of words that includes *communion*, *communism* and *community*. Until you have shared information with another person, you haven't communicated it. And until they have understood it, the way you understand it, you haven't shared it with them.

Communication is the process of creating shared understanding.

how people understand

Another definition: communication is displaying the shape of a person's thinking.

Different people understand the same information differently. One person might recognise the words and pictures immediately; to another, they might be in a foreign language (double Dutch, perhaps, or 'all Greek'). Every communication problem is a problem of understanding.

Understanding is recognition. 'Ah!' you exclaim when you've understood something, 'I *see*!' People talk a lot about looking when describing the way they understand. You may have a different *perspective* on a problem from a colleague; you may misunderstand each other because you are both approaching the issue from different *angles*. If you disagree with someone, you may say that you *are looking* at it differently.

People understand information that they recognise. I understand that the vehicle approaching me is a bus, because I've seen one before. I understand a tune because I've heard it – or tunes like it – before. I understand I'm eating chicken paprika because I recognise the taste. Similarly, I will understand what you are telling me if it fits a mental pattern that I already have.

Understanding, then, is fitting what you're looking at into your mental patterns. If you want to communicate well, you must make the shape of your thinking visible. How could you do that? You could draw pictures or patterns on paper. You might ask the other person to imagine a pattern and then fit your information into that. It would certainly help if you simplified the information, so that the shape of your thinking isn't obscured by detail.

managing information

Your success as a manager increasingly depends on your ability to manage information.

We think of information as 'stuff' that comes in 'bits'. Those bits are 'out there': you can see them, measure them, and count them. Understanding is thought of as the process of 'printing' this information on the mind. We imagine the mind to be like a computer's hard disk. It has a certain capacity, a fixed amount of available space for incoming information. Too much input and you suffer from 'information overload'. If information overload persists, the system might 'crash'.

Now, most people know that this isn't how information actually works. Every time people communicate, information takes on a different meaning. That's what information is like. Children have enormous fun playing with the way information can alter in the telling. Chinese Whispers and Charades are both games that delightfully exploit people's capacity to misunderstand each other.

In fact, information is what you *create* inside your head as you understand. Information is never 'out there'; it is always, and only ever, in the mind. Information is the shape of your thinking. And the shape of information is constantly changing, evolving, as you think. Information is dynamic. Every time you communicate, information transforms itself as you filter it through the mental patterns in your mind. Communication is always a game of Chinese Whispers.

At work, people try to treat information as 'stuff' and try to file it, process it, collate it, record it and store it – even if they don't understand it. Information is expected to be controllable, stable, and manageable.

But the project is doomed to failure. Information can never be controlled, fixed, contained. It's not a commodity; it's energy. Information is food for thought; it's the source of vitality in organisations. Ration it and people will find anything to survive. Rumour, hearsay, scandal, gossip, the 'grapevine' – these are all 'junk food' people use to stay alive when they lack the real thing.

Once you see information as energy, rather than 'stuff', you can manage it differently. What matters now is not *how much* information you communicate, but what form it takes. And the *form* of information is its *meaning*.

Communication is never a matter of handing over a bundle of information; it is a matter of creating *meaning* out of that information, and then sharing that meaning. If the other person can't understand what you mean, then your attempts to communicate have failed.

Think of that glass containing 50 per cent of the amount of water it can hold. What does this information *mean*? That the glass is half empty? Or that it's half full? The meaning you give the information dictates the information you communicate.

Communication is creating shared meaning. So, how do we create meaning? By turning information into ideas.

ideas: the currency of communication

Communication is the process of creating and sharing clear ideas. Effective communication depends, not on the accuracy of your facts, but on the richness of your ideas. Indeed, the whole process of communication could be defined as creating shared ideas.

What do I mean by an idea? I mean something specific. An idea is something you say (or write) about something. A name is not an idea. The following phrases are all names but, for the purposes of this exercise, they aren't ideas:

- profit analysis;
- Asian market;
- operations director.

To turn them into ideas, you have to say something about them, for example:

- Profit analysis shows an upturn in sales of consumables over the past year.
- The Asian market has become unstable.
- Bill Freeman is now operations director.

We've created a sentence. An idea, then, is *any thought that can be expressed in a sentence.*

An idea doesn't have to be new. When you say 'I've got an idea', you usually mean that this is an idea nobody has had before. Most ideas, of course, aren't entirely new. Every time anyone utters a sentence, they are uttering an idea.

Ideas are the currency of communication. When people communicate, they trade ideas. Like currency, ideas come in larger or smaller denominations: there are big ideas, and little ideas. The little ones can be assembled into larger units, by summarising them. Like currencies, ideas have a value and that value can change: some ideas become more valuable as others lose their value. The value of an idea is in its meaning. Ideas are judged differently from facts. The quality of a fact is judged by how accurate it is. The quality of an idea is judged by how *meaningful* it is.

When communication fails, it's because someone doesn't understand an idea. Perhaps the person can't see its value. Perhaps there are too many ideas. Perhaps the idea has become lost in a sea of facts and figures. You may hint at an idea if you are uncertain how the other person will receive it. Your voice may utter one idea but your face may hint at another.

The most effective communication makes ideas explicit. Your purpose in communicating is to create and share clear ideas.

conversation: the heart of communication

Conversation is the stock exchange where we trade ideas. It's the most important means of communication you possess. It is flexible and dynamic. Your organisation – any organisation – is, in essence, a network of conversations. In fact, that's all it is. Without effective conversations, it cannot operate.

Conversations are the way we create shared meaning. All the other ways of communicating – interviews, presentations, written documents – are variations on this central mode of communication. If you want to communicate better, begin by improving your conversations.

how conversations work

Conversation is your primary management tool. It's how you plan your life and organise your work. It's how you build relationships with colleagues and customers. It's how you come to understand how people feel, what they think and what they are doing. Conversation is the way you influence others and are influenced by them. It's how you solve problems, co-operate with others and create new opportunities.

Maybe the old saying is true, that conversation is a dying art. Research has shown that six out of ten people in the UK want to be able to hold better conversations.

I can believe it. In most of the organisations I visit as a consultant, people are desperate to recover some part of the satisfaction of conversation. A manager summed up the dilemma neatly to me recently. 'If we don't re-learn how to talk with each other', he said, 'frequently and on a meaningful level, this organisation won't survive.'

what is a conversation?

Conversations are verbal dances. The word derives from the

Latin 'to move around with'. Like any dance, a conversation has rules, and standard moves. These allow people to move more harmoniously together, without stepping on each other's toes or getting out of step. Different kinds of conversation have different conventions. Some are implicitly understood; others – for example in presentations or meetings – must be spelt out in detail and rehearsed.

A conversation is a dynamic of talking and listening. You may think of conversations as people talking to each other; they are also people listening to each other. Without the listening, there's no conversation. These two activities occur simultaneously. Each participant in a conversation is both a speaker and a listener.

The quality of conversation depends more on the quality of the listening than on the quality of the speaking. Listening is the way you find out what the other person means and how they think. It's by listening that you find the common ground, the shared understanding that the two of you are seeking.

If you want to improve your conversation, a good place to start is with your listening skills. Listening is more than just not speaking, and more than hearing. The listener controls the speaker's behaviour by the way they listen: by maintaining eye contact, by their body position, by nodding or shaking their head, by taking notes and so on. You demonstrate the quality of your listening whenever you speak. If you make a remark that the other person sees as irrelevant, they begin to doubt whether you have listened carefully. If you interrupt, you show that you don't want to listen.

balancing advocacy and inquiry

Peter Senge, author of *The Fifth Discipline*, uses the words 'advocacy' and 'inquiry' to describe talking and listening. Talking is principally the means by which you advocate your point of view. Listening is the process of enquiring into the other person's point of view.

Advocacy without inquiry can escalate into conflict. Conflict can be so upsetting that managers avoid holding conversations at all and retreat behind their office door – if they are lucky enough to have one.

But conversations that are pure inquiry are also unsatisfactory. If you concentrate solely on listening to the other person, you risk an unclear outcome – or no outcome at all. Indeed, some managers use the skills of inquiry – listening, asking questions, and always looking for the other point of view – as a way of avoiding difficult decisions.

The best conversations balance advocacy and inquiry. They are a rich mix of talking and listening, of stating views and asking questions.

why conversations go wrong

Everyone can think of conversations at work that have gone wrong. Working out *why* they went wrong may be hard. Conversations are so subtle and they happen so fast. Few people have been trained in the art of effective conversation. Conversation is a life skill, and – like most life skills – one that you are usually expected to pick up as you go along.

The reasons why conversations fail might be grouped under the following four headings:

- context;
- relationship;
- structure;
- behaviour.

These are the four dimensions of conversation. By looking at them, we can begin to understand more clearly how conversations work, why they go wrong, and how to begin to improve them.

putting conversations in context

All conversations have a context. They happen for a reason. Most conversations form part of a process or a developing relationship. No conversation happens in an information vacuum.

Many conversations fail because one or both speakers ignore the context. If you don't check why the conversation is happening, each of you may very quickly start to misunderstand the other.

The problem may simply be that the conversation never happens. One of the most persistent complaints against managers is that they are not there to talk to: 'I never see him'; 'she has no idea what I do'; 'he simply refuses to listen'. Other obvious problems that afflict the context of the conversation include:

- not giving enough time to the conversation;
- holding the conversation at the wrong time;
- conversing in an uncomfortable, busy or noisy place;
- a lack of privacy.

Less obvious, but just as important, are the assumptions that we bring to our conversations. If you leave these assumptions unquestioned, misunderstandings and conflict can quickly arise. For example, you might assume that:

- you both know what you are talking about;
- you need to agree;
- you know how the other person views the situation;
- you shouldn't let your feelings show;
- the other person is somehow to blame for the problem;
- you can be brutally honest;
- you need to solve the other person's problem;
- you're right and they're wrong.

There may be deeper assumptions lying beneath these assumptions: about the nature of the problem, about what kind of business you are in, about your role as a manager. The more you think about the assumptions that underlie conversations, the more seem to emerge!

These assumptions derive from your *mental models*: about what is true, or about what you – or others – should do. For example, you might hold a mental model that you are in business to make a profit; that women have an inherently different management style from men; or that character is determined by some set of national characteristics. Millions of mental models shape and drive people's thinking, all the time. It's not possible to think *without* mental models. Thinking is the process of developing and changing mental models.

All too often, however, conversations become conflicts between these mental models. Instead of achieving a useful or productive outcome, you try to use your own mental model to beat the other person into submission. This is adversarial conversation, and it is one of the most important and deadly reasons why conversations go wrong. (You'll find more about adversarial conversation in Chapter 3.)

---

key factors: context

- ▪ **Objectives.** Do you both know why you are holding the conversation?
- ▪ **Time.** Is this the right time to be holding this conversation? What is the history behind the conversation? Is it part of a larger process?
- ▪ **Place.** Are you conversing in a place that is comfortable, quiet, and free from distractions?
- ▪ **Assumptions.** Do you both understand the assumptions that you are starting from? Do you need to explore them before going further?

working out the relationship

The relationship defines the limits and potential of our conversation. We converse differently with complete strangers than with close acquaintances. A difficult relationship may cause us to speak in code. Conversations are ways of establishing, fixing or changing a relationship.

Relationships are neither fixed nor permanent. They are complex and dynamic. Relationships operate along a number of dimensions, including:

■ status;
■ power;
■ role;
■ liking.

All of these factors help to define the territory of the conversation. You enter the conversation on your own territory. Part of any conversation is the definition of that territory and negotiation about whether the other person is welcome there. You might want to ask permission to enter the other person's territory; you might equally invite or refuse them access to yours.

status

Status is the rank you grant to another person in relation to you. It is normally measured along a simple (some might say simplistic) scale. You see yourself simply as higher or lower in status in relation to the other person.

People confer status on others. It's evident in the degree of respect, familiarity or reserve people have for each other. A person's own sense of status comes from the status that others give them.

Status regulates conversations. If you feel you have a lower status than another person, you may agree to everything the other person says and suppress strongly held ideas of your own. If you feel you have a higher status than someone else, you may discount what they say, put them down, interrupt or even ignore them. Indeed, these behaviours are ways of establishing or altering someone's status in a relationship.

Status is always at risk. It is created entirely through the other person's perceptions. It can be destroyed or diminished in a moment.

power

Power is the control people exert over each other. If you can influence or control someone's behaviour in any way, you have power over them. John French and Bertram Raven, in the late 1950s, identified five kinds of power base:

- reward power – the ability to grant favours for behaviour;
- coercive power – the ability to punish others;
- legitimate power – conferred by law or other sets of rules;
- referent power – the 'charisma' that causes others to imitate or idolise;
- expert power – deriving from specific levels of knowledge or skill.

Conversations often fail because they become power struggles. People may seek to exercise different kinds of power at different points in a conversation. If you have little reward power over the other person, for example, you may try to influence them as an expert. If you lack charisma or respect for the other person, you may try to exert authority by appealing to legitimate or to coercive power.

Seduction is another way in which power afflicts conversations. Seduction means that you end up doing something you hadn't intended. The other person has used their power to seduce you away from what you wanted to talk about towards their area of interest. Conversational seduction – like other kinds of seduction – usually happens because it's pleasurable. You frequently end up, however, discussing matters of little importance and finish the conversation without having achieved your goal.

role

A role is a set of behaviours that people expect of each other. A formal role may be explicitly defined in a job description; an informal role is conferred on you as a result of people's experience of your conversations.

People tend to converse with each other in role. If the other person knows that your formal role is an accountant, for example, they will tend to converse with you in that role. If they know that your informal role is usually the devil's advocate, or mediator, or licensed fool, they will adapt their conversation to that role. You may have heard of Meredith Belbin's list of team roles. Thousands of managers have now used Belbin's questionnaire to locate themselves among his categories of:

- chair/co-ordinator;
- shaper/team leader;
- plant/innovator or creative thinker;
- monitor-evaluator/critical thinker;
- company worker/implementer;
- team worker/team builder;
- finisher/detail checker and pusher;
- resource investigator/researcher outside the team;
- expert.

A particular danger of such analysis is that people will label themselves with a role and start to operate exclusively within it. The conversations that result will tend to be limited by the perceived roles that are operating.

liking

Conversations can fail because the speakers dislike each other. But they can also go wrong because they like each other a lot! The simple distinction between liking and disliking seems crude. You can find people attractive in many different ways or not take to them in ways you may not be able – or willing – to articulate. Liking can become an emotional entanglement or even a fully fledged relationship; dislike can turn into a vendetta.

These four factors affect the territorial relationship in the conversation. A successful conversation seeks out the shared territory: the common ground between people. But people guard their own territory carefully. As a result, many conversational rules are about how to invite and give permission for another person to enter our personal territory. You may tiptoe around the borders of an issue because you are uncertain whether you would be welcome on that part of another person's territory. You can also feel invaded if the other person broaches a matter that you feel is out of bounds to them.

The success of a conversation may depend on whether you give or ask clearly for such permission. People often ask for or give permission in code. Often, it's only when the person reacts that you realise you have intruded on private territory. The misunderstandings that result from such territorial disputes or skirmishes can destroy a conversation.

---

key factors: relationship

■ **Status.** Is there a marked difference in status between you? Why is that? How does this difference affect the way you are behaving towards the other person? How do you think it might be affecting their behaviour?

■ **Power.** Can you see power being wielded in the conversation? What kind of power? In which direction?

How might you both be affecting the power relationship? How do you want to affect it?

■ **Role.** What is your role in this conversation? Think about your formal role (your job title, perhaps, or contractual position) and your informal role. How do people see you acting in conversations? Can you feel yourself falling naturally into any particular role in the conversation?

■ **Liking.** How is the conversation being affected by your feelings towards each other? Is the liking or disliking getting in the way of a productive outcome?

■ **Territory.** Where are the boundaries? Are you finding common ground? Where can you give permission for the other person to enter your territory? Where can you ask permission to enter theirs?

setting a structure

Many conversations are a mess. People rush. They wander from point to point. They repeat themselves. They get stuck in a groove. Some conversations proceed in parallel, with each person telling their own story or making their own points with no reference to what the other person is saying. If conversation is a verbal dance, people often find themselves trying to dance two different dances at the same time, or treading on each other's toes.

Why should you worry about the structure of your conversations? After all, conversations are supposed to be living and flexible. Wouldn't a structure make your conversation too rigid and uncomfortable?

Maybe. But all living organisms have structures. They cannot grow and develop healthily unless they conform to fundamental structuring principles. Conversations, too, have structural principles. You can develop the quality of your conversation by recognising these structures and making them even more sophisticated.

The structure of a conversation derives from the way people think. Think about thinking as a two-stage process:

- **First-stage thinking** is the thinking you do when you are looking at reality. It allows you to recognise something because it fits into some mental model or idea. Ideas allow you to make sense of reality, and it is this sense-making that is first-stage thinking. The result of first-stage thinking is that you translate reality into language. You name an object or an event; you turn a complicated physical process into an equation; you simplify a structure by drawing a diagram; you contain a landscape on a map.
- **Second-stage thinking** manipulates the language you have created to achieve a result. Having named something as, say, a cup, you can talk about it coherently. You can judge its effectiveness as a cup, its value to you, how you might use it or how you might improve its design. Having labelled a downturn in sales as a marketing problem, you explore the consequences in marketing terms.

All conversations follow this simple structure. You cannot talk about anything until you have named it. Conversely, how you name something determines the way you talk about it. The quality of your second-stage thinking depends directly on the quality of your first-stage thinking.

We are very good at second-stage thinking. Everyone has lots of experience in manipulating language. They are so good at it that they can build machines to do it for them: computers are very fast manipulators of binary language.

We aren't nearly so good at first-stage thinking. We name things without thinking. The cup is obviously a cup; who would dream of calling it anything else? The marketing problem is obviously a marketing problem – isn't it? As a result, most conversations complete the first stage in a few seconds. People leap to making judgements.

Suppose the cup was named as – to take a few possibilities at random – a chalice, or a vase, or a trophy. Your second-stage thinking about that object would change radically. Suppose you decided that the marketing problem might be a production problem, a distribution problem or a personnel problem. You would start to think very differently about it at the second stage.

Effective conversations have a first stage and a second stage. People prefer to take their perceptions for granted. But no amount of second-stage thinking will make up for faulty or limited first-stage thinking. Good thinking pays attention to both stages.

An effective conversation manages structure by:

▨ separating the two stages;
▨ checking that you both know what stage you are in;
▨ asking the questions appropriate to each stage.

---

key factors: structure

Each stage of the conversation includes key questions. Use these questions to develop your thinking in each stage.

First-stage thinking
▨ What do you want to achieve?
▨ What are you looking at?
▨ What might it mean?
▨ How else could you look at it?
▨ What else could you call it?
▨ How would someone else see it?
▨ What is it like?

Second-stage thinking
▨ What do you think about this?
▨ How do you evaluate it?
▨ What can you do?
▨ What opportunities are there?
▨ How useful is it?
▨ Why are you interested in this?
▨ How does this fit in with your plans?
▨ What are you going to do?

managing behaviour

Conversations are never simply exchanges of words. Supporting the language you use is a whole range of *non-verbal communication*: the tone of your voice; the gestures you use; the way you move your eyes or hold your body; the physical positions you adopt in relation to the other person. Much of this behaviour is perceived unconsciously. The information you pick up from the other person's non-verbal communication influences your response *more* than the words they use.

Bodies leak information. You have less control over your non-verbal behaviour than over the way you speak. This may be because you have learnt most of your body language implicitly, by absorbing and imitating the body language of people around you. Your non-verbal communication will sometimes say things to the other person that you don't intend them to know.

Non-verbal communication is important for the following reasons:

■ Non-verbal messages communicate feelings – they are the primary way of expressing emotions or instinctive reactions.

■ Non-verbal messages are seen as more reliable than verbal ones – they are less easy to fake.

■ Non-verbal communication means that it is impossible not to communicate – every kind of behaviour in relation to the other person communicates something.

■ Non-verbal messages relate strongly to verbal messages – they may reinforce, regulate, emphasise, contradict or substitute for the words people use.

Conversations often go wrong because people misinterpret non-verbal messages. There are four main reasons for this:

■ **Non-verbal messages are ambiguous.** No dictionary can accurately define them. Their meaning can vary according to context, to the degree of intention in giving them, and because they may not consistently reflect feeling. Some people close their eyes to concentrate on what you are saying; others do so to try to avoid paying you attention.

■ **Non-verbal messages are continuous.** You can stop talking but you can't stop behaving! Language is bound by the structures of grammar so that you can tell if an idea has finished and when the speaker is starting a new one. Non-verbal communication is not structured in the same way.

■ **Non-verbal messages are multichannel.** Everything is happening at once: eyes, hands, feet, body position. Non-verbal messages are interpreted holistically, as a whole impression. This makes them strong but unspecific, so you may not be able to pin down exactly why you get the impression you do.

■ **Non-verbal messages are culturally determined.** Research suggests that a few non-verbal messages are universal: everybody seems to smile when they are happy, for example. Most non-verbal behaviours, however, are specific to a culture. A lot of confusion can arise from the misinterpretation of non-verbal messages across a cultural divide.

The best-known research into non-verbal communication is probably Albert Mehrabian's work in the late 1960s. In his book *Silent Messages* (1971) Mehrabian suggests that people communicate far more through tone of voice and facial expression than they do with the actual words spoken. He even put numbers on this idea. 'Total feeling', he suggested, is made up of '7 per cent verbal feeling, 38 per cent vocal feeling and 55 per cent facial feeling'. Others have found these numbers difficult to take seriously, and have challenged the way Mehrabian worked them out. Nonetheless, there are important general lessons to learn from Mehrabian. You say more non-verbally than you do with words. If your non-verbal behaviour contradicts the words you use, the other person will probably believe the non-verbal communication.

Effective communicators manage their behaviour. They work hard to align their non-verbal messages with their words. Actors, of course, develop behaviour management into an art. You may feel that trying to manage your own behaviour in the same way is dishonest: 'play-acting' a part that you don't necessarily feel. But everyone acts when they hold a conversation. Managing your behaviour simply means trying to act appropriately.

The most important things to manage are eye contact and body movement. Simple actions like keeping your limbs and hands still, or looking steadily at the speaker while they are speaking, can make a big and immediate difference to the quality of the conversation.

key factors: managing behaviour

- **Check the context.** Don't try to interpret non-verbal messages in isolation from any others, or from the wider situation. Folded arms may mean that someone is hostile to your ideas, or that they are cold.

- **Look for clusters.** If you are picking up a group of non-verbal messages that seem to indicate a single feeling, you may be able to trust your interpretation more fully.

- **Consider past experience.** You can interpret more accurately the behaviour of people you know. You certainly notice *changes* in their behaviour. You also interpret patterns of behaviour over time more accurately than single instances.

- **Check your perceptions.** Ask questions. You are interpreting observed behaviour, not reading someone's mind. Check out what you observe and make sure that your interpretation is accurate.

seven ways to improve your conversations

Your success as a manager depends on your ability to hold effective and productive conversations. This chapter looks at seven proven strategies to help you improve your conversations:

- Clarify your objective.
- Structure your thinking.
- Manage your time.
- Find common ground.
- Move beyond argument.
- Summarise often.
- Use visuals.

Don't feel that you must apply all seven at once. Take a single strategy and work at it for a few days. (You should have plenty of conversations to practise on!) Once you feel that you have integrated that skill into your conversations, move on to another.

clarify your objective

Work out at the start of your conversation what you want to achieve. People often find themselves starting a conversation without knowing its objective. Somebody starts chatting to you at the coffee machine. Is this just chatting, or is there more to it? How will you know their objective? Only if they tell you. If they launch into the conversation in the middle of their own thinking, you'll spend time trying to piece it all together and actually missing a good deal of what they say. Worst of all, *you* may start a conversation without knowing why. You may have a mass of concerns on your mind, lots of things you want to say, but no clear focus on what you want to *achieve*.

Think of a conversation as a journey you are taking together. It will very quickly start to wander off track if either of you is unclear where you're going. You will complete the journey effectively only if you both know clearly where you are aiming for.

What's vital is that you *state* your objective clearly at the start. Give a headline. If you know what your main point is, state it at the start of the conversation. That way, the other person is better prepared to make sense of everything else you say. Of course, you'll be able to give a headline much more easily if you have thought about it beforehand.

---

headlines

Newspapers rely on headlines to get the story's message across quickly. You can do the same in your conversations:

> I want to talk to you about...
> I've looked at the plan and I've got some suggestions.
> I know you're worried about the sales figures. I've got some clues that might help.
> I've called this meeting to make a decision about project X.

Of course, you might decide to change your objective in the middle of the conversation – just as you might decide to change direction in the middle of a journey. That's fine, so long as both of you know what you're doing. Too specific an objective at the start might limit your success at the end. This problem is at the heart of negotiation, for example: what would you be willing to settle for, and what is not negotiable?

Objectives roughly divide into two categories:

■ exploring a problem;
■ finding a solution.

When you are thinking about your headline, ask 'problem or solution?' Being able to distinguish between these two kinds of objective is a vital conversational skill. You may tend to assume that any conversation about a problem is aiming to find a solution – particularly if the other person has started the conversation. As a result, you may find yourself working towards a solution without accurately defining or understanding the problem. It may be that the other person doesn't *want* you to offer a solution, but rather to talk through the problem with them.

structure your thinking

You can improve your conversations enormously by giving them structure. The simplest way to structure a conversation is to break it in half.

Thinking can be seen as a two-stage process. *First-stage thinking* is thinking about a problem; *second-stage thinking* is thinking about a solution.

Many managerial conversations leap to second-stage thinking without spending nearly enough time in the first stage. They look for solutions and almost ignore the problem.

Why this urge to ignore the problem? Perhaps because problems are frightening. To stay with a problem – to explore it, to try to understand it further, to confront it and live with it for a few moments – is too uncomfortable. People don't like living with unresolved problems. Better to deal with it: sort it out; solve it; get rid of it.

Resist the temptation to rush into second-stage thinking. Give the first stage – the problem stage – as much attention and time as you think appropriate. Then give it a little more. And make sure that you are both in the same stage of the conversation at the same time.

Link the stages of your conversation together. Linking helps you to steer the conversation comfortably. Skilled conversation holders can steer the conversation by linking the following:

- the past and the present;
- the problem and the solution;
- first-stage and second-stage thinking;
- requests and answers;
- negative ideas and positive ideas;
- opinions about what is true, with speculation about the consequences.

WASP: welcome; acquire; supply; part

In my early days as a manager, I was introduced to a simple four-stage model of conversation that I still use. It breaks down the two stages of thinking into four steps:

- **Welcome (first-stage thinking).** At the start of the conversation, state your objectives, set the scene and establish your relationship: 'Why are we talking about this matter? Why *us*?'
- **Acquire (first-stage thinking).** The second step is information gathering. Concentrate on finding out as much as possible about the matter, from as many angles as

you can. For both of you, listening is vital. You are acquiring knowledge from each other. This part of the conversation should be dominated by questions.

■ **Supply (second-stage thinking).** Now, at the third step, we summarise what we've learnt and begin to work out what to do with the information. We are beginning to think about how we might move forward: the options that present themselves. It's important at this stage of the conversation to remind yourselves of the objective that you set at the start.

■ **Part (second-stage thinking).** Finally, you work out what you have agreed. You state explicitly the conversation's outcome: the action that will result from it. The essence of the parting stage is that you explicitly agree what is going to happen next. What is going to happen? Who will do it? Is there a deadline? Who is going to check on progress?

From impromptu conversations in the corridor to formal interviews, WASP gives you a simple framework to make sure that the conversation stays on track and results in a practical outcome.

four types of conversation

This simple four-stage model can become more sophisticated. In this developed model, you hold four conversations, for:

■ relationship;
■ possibility;
■ opportunity;
■ action.

These four conversations may form part of a single, larger conversation; they may also take place separately, at different stages of a process or project.

a conversation for relationship ('welcome')

You hold a conversation for relationship to create or develop the relationship you need to achieve your objective. It is an exploration.

---

a conversation for relationship: key questions

Who are we?
How do we relate to the matter in hand?
What links us?
How do we see things?
What do you see that I can't see?
What do I see that you don't see?
In what ways do we see things similarly, or differently?
How can we understand each other?
Where do we stand?
Can we stand together?

Conversations for relationship are tentative and sometimes awkward. They are often rushed because they can be embarrassing. Think of those tricky conversations you have had with strangers at parties: they are good examples of conversations for relationship. A managerial conversation for relationship should move beyond the 'What do you do? Where do you live?' questions. You are defining your relationship to each other, and to the matter in hand.

a conversation for possibility ('acquire')

A conversation for possibility continues the exploration: it develops first-stage thinking. It asks what you *might* be looking at.

A conversation for possibility is *not* about whether to do something, or what to do. It seeks to find new ways of looking at the problem.

There are a number of ways of doing this:

- Look at it from a new angle.
- Ask for different interpretations of what's happening.
- Try to distinguish what you're looking at from what you think about it.
- Ask how other people might see it.
- Break the problem into parts.
- Isolate one part of the problem and look at it in detail.
- Connect the problem into a wider network of ideas.
- Ask what the problem is like. What does it look like, or feel like?

Conversations for possibility are potentially a source of creativity: brainstorming is a good example. But they can also be uncomfortable: exploring different points of view may create conflict.

a conversation for possibility: key questions

What's the problem?
What are we trying to do?
What's the real problem?
What are we really trying to do?
Is this a problem?
How could we look at this from a different angle?
Can we interpret this differently?
How could we do this?
What does it look like from another person's point of view?
What makes this different from last time?
Have we ever done anything like this before?
Can we make this simpler?
Can we look at this in bits?
What is this like?
What does this feel or look like?

Manage this conversation with care. Make it clear that this is not decision time. Encourage the other person to give you ideas. Take care not to judge or criticise. Do challenge or probe what the other person says. In particular, manage the emotional content of this conversation with care. Acknowledge people's feelings and look for the evidence that supports them.

a conversation for opportunity ('supply')

A conversation for opportunity takes us into second-stage thinking. This is fundamentally a conversation about planning. Many good ideas never become reality because people don't map out paths of opportunity. A conversation for opportunity is designed to construct such a path. You are choosing what to do. You assess what you would need to make action possible: resources, support and skills. This conversation is more focused than a conversation for possibility: in choosing from among a number of possibilities, you are finding a sense of common purpose.

---

a conversation for opportunity: key questions

Where can we act?
What could we do?
Which possibilities do we build on?
Which possibilities are feasible?
What target do we set ourselves?
Where are the potential obstacles?
How will we know that we've succeeded?

The bridge from possibility to opportunity is *measurement*. This is where you begin to set targets, milestones, obstacles, measures of success. How will you be able to judge when you have achieved an objective?

Recall your original objective. Has it changed? Conversations for opportunity can become more exciting by placing yourselves in a future where you have achieved your objective. What does such a future look and feel like? What is happening in this future? How can you plan your way towards it? Most people plan by starting from where they are and extrapolate current actions towards a desired objective. By 'backward planning' from an imagined future, you can find new opportunities for action.

a conversation for action ('part')

This is where you agree what to do, who will do it and when it will happen. Translating opportunity into action needs more than agreement; you need to generate a promise, a commitment to act.

Managers often remark that getting action is one of the hardest aspects of managing people. 'Have you noticed', one senior director said to me recently, 'how people seem never to do what they've agreed to do?' Following up on agreed actions can become a major time-waster. A conversation for action is the first step in pre-empting the problem. It's vital that the promise resulting from a conversation for action is recorded.

---

a conversation for action: key stages

A conversation for action is a dynamic between asking and promising. It takes a specific form:

▓ You ask the other person to do something by a certain time. Make it clear that this is a request, not an order. Orders may get immediate results, but they rarely generate commitment.

▓ The other person has four possible answers to this request.

- They can accept.
- They can decline.
- They may commit to accepting or declining at a later date ('I'll let you know by x').
- They can make a counter-offer ('I can't do that, but I can do x').

▓ The conversation results in a promise ('I will do x for you by time y').

This four-stage model of conversation – either in its simple WASP form, or in the more sophisticated form of relationship-possibility-opportunity-action – will serve you well in the wide range of conversations you will hold as a manager. Some of your conversations will include all four stages; some will concentrate on one more than another.

These conversations will only be truly effective if you hold them *in order*. The success of each conversation depends on the success of the conversation before it. If you fail to resolve a conversation, it will continue underneath the next *in code*. Unresolved aspects of a conversation for relationship, for instance, can become conflicts of possibility, hidden agendas or 'personality clashes'. Possibilities left unexplored become lost opportunities. And promises to act that have no real commitment behind them will create problems later.

manage your time

Conversations take time, and time is the one entirely non-renewable resource. It's vital that you manage time well, both for and in your conversations.

managing time for the conversation

Work out how much time you have. Don't just assume that there is no time. Be realistic. If necessary, make an appointment at another time to hold the conversation. Make sure it's a time that both of you find convenient.

managing time in the conversation

Most conversations proceed at a varying rate. Generally, an effective conversation will probably start quite slowly and get faster as it goes on. But there are no real rules about this.

You know that a conversation is going too fast when people interrupt each other a lot, when parallel conversations start, when people stop listening to each other and when people start to show signs of becoming uncomfortable. Conversations can go too fast because:

- we become solution-oriented;
- feelings take over;
- we succumb to 'groupthink' (everybody starts thinking alike to reinforce the group);
- we're enjoying ourselves too much;
- assumptions go unchallenged;
- people stop asking questions;
- arguments flare up.

Conversely, you know that a conversation is slowing down when one person starts to dominate the conversation, when questions dry up, when people pause a lot, when the energy level in the conversation starts to drop or when people show signs of weariness. Conversations start to slow down because:

- the conversation becomes problem-centred;
- too much analysis is going on;
- people talk more about the past than the future;
- more and more questions are asked;
- people start to repeat themselves;
- the conversation wanders;
- people hesitate before saying anything.

Try to become aware of how fast the conversation is proceeding, and how fast you think it *should* be going. Here are some simple tactics to help you regain control of time in your conversations.

If you feel that the conversation is speeding up, try the following:

▩ Reflect what the other person says rather than replying directly to it.

▩ Summarise their remark before moving on to your own.

▩ Ask open questions (questions that can't be answered by 'yes' or 'no'.

If you feel that the conversation is slowing down try the following:

▩ Push for action: 'What shall we *do*?' 'What do you propose doing?'. Signal that you are looking for action, not words.

▩ Summarise and link the points of the conversation together, so that you can bring one stage of thinking to a conclusion and move on to the next.

▩ Look for the implications of what the other person is saying: 'What does that mean in terms of...?' 'How does this affect our plans?' 'So what action is possible here?'.

▩ Ask for new ideas and offer some new ones of your own.

find common ground

Conversations are ways of finding common ground. You mostly begin in your own private territory and use the conversation to find boundaries and the openings where you can cross over to the other person's ground.

Notice how you ask for, and give, permission for these moves to happen. If you are asking permission to move into new territory, you might:

■ make a remark tentatively;
■ express yourself with lots of hesitant padding: 'perhaps we might...', 'I suppose I think...', 'It's possible that...';
■ pause before speaking;
■ look away or down a lot;
■ explicitly ask permission: 'Do you mind if I mention...', 'May I speak freely about...'.

You do not proceed until the other person has given their permission. Such permission may be explicit: 'Please say what you like'; 'I would really welcome your honest opinion'; 'I don't mind you talking about that'. Other signs of permission might be in the person's body language or behaviour: nodding, smiling, leaning forward.

Conversely, refusing permission can be explicit – 'I'd rather we didn't talk about this' – or in code. The person may evade your question, wrap up an answer in clouds of mystification or reply with another question. Their non-verbal behaviour is more likely to give you a hint of their real feelings: folding their arms, sitting back in the chair, becoming restless, evading eye contact.

move beyond argument

One of the most effective ways of improving your conversations is to work at developing them beyond argument.

Most people are better at talking than at listening. At school, we learn the skills of *debate*: of taking a position, holding it, defending it, convincing others of its worth and attacking any position that threatens it.

As a result, conversations have a habit of becoming *adversarial*. Instead of searching out the common ground, people hold their own corner and treat every move by the other person as an attack. Adversarial conversations set up a boxing match between competing opinions.

Opinions are ideas gone cold. They are assumptions about what should be true, rather than conclusions about what is true in specific circumstances. Opinions might include:

- stories (about what happened, what may have happened, why it happened);
- explanations (of why something went wrong, why it failed);
- justifications for doing what was done;
- gossip (perhaps to make someone feel better at the expense of others);
- generalisations (to save the bother of thinking);
- wrong-making (to establish power over the other person).

Opinions are often mistaken for the truth. Whenever you hear someone – maybe yourself – saying that something is 'a well-established fact', you can be certain that they are voicing an opinion.

Adversarial conversation stops the truth from emerging. Arguing actually stops you exploring and discovering ideas. And the quality of the conversation rapidly worsens: people are too busy defending themselves, too frightened and too battle-fatigued to do any better.

the Ladder of Inference

The Ladder of Inference is a powerful model that helps you move beyond argument. It was developed initially by Chris

Argyris. He pictures the way people think in conversations as a ladder. At the bottom of the ladder is observation; at the top, action.

■ From your observation, you step on to the first rung of the ladder by selecting *data*. (You choose what to look at.)
■ On the second rung, you infer *meaning* from your experience of similar data.
■ On the third rung, you generalise those meanings into *assumptions*.
■ On the fourth rung, you construct mental models (or *beliefs*) out of those assumptions.
■ You act on the basis of your mental models.

You travel up and down this ladder whenever you hold a conversation. You are much better at climbing up than stepping down. In fact, you can leap up all the rungs in a few seconds. These 'leaps of abstraction' allow you to act more quickly, but they can also limit the course of the conversation. Even more worryingly, your mental models help you to select data from future observation, further limiting the range of the conversation. This is a 'reflexive loop'; you might call it a mindset.

The Ladder of Inference gives you more choices about where to go in a conversation. It helps you to *slow down* your thinking. It allows you to:

■ become more aware of your own thinking;
■ make that thinking available to the other person;
■ ask them about their thinking.

Above all, it allows you to defuse an adversarial conversation by 'climbing down' from private beliefs, assumptions and opinions, and then 'climbing up' to shared meanings and beliefs.

The key to using the Ladder of Inference is to ask questions. This helps you to find the differences in the way people think, what they have in common and how they might reach shared understanding.

- ▨ What's the data that underlies what you've said?
- ▨ Do we agree on the data?
- ▨ Do we agree on what they mean?
- ▨ Can you take me through your reasoning?
- ▨ When you say [what you've said], do you mean [my rewording of it]?

For example, if someone suggests a particular course of action, you can carefully climb down the ladder by asking:

- ▨ 'Why do you think this might work?' 'What makes this a good plan?'
- ▨ 'What assumptions do you think you might be making?' 'Have you considered...?'
- ▨ 'How would this affect...?' 'Does this mean that...?'
- ▨ 'Can you give me an example?' 'What led you to look at this in particular?'

Even more powerfully, the Ladder of Inference can help you to offer your own thinking for the other person to examine. If you are suggesting a plan of action, you can ask:

- ▨ 'Can you see any flaws in my thinking?'
- ▨ 'Would you look at this stuff differently?' 'How would you put this together?'
- ▨ 'Would this look different in different circumstances?' 'Are my assumptions valid?'
- ▨ 'Have I missed anything?'

The beauty of this model is that you need no special training to use it. Neither does the other participant in the conversation. You can use it immediately, as a practical way to intervene in conversations that are collapsing into argument.

summarise often

Perhaps the most important of all the skills of conversation is the skill of summarising.

- Summaries allow you to state your objective, return to it and check that you have achieved it.
- Summaries help you to structure your thinking.
- Summaries help you to manage time more effectively.
- Summaries help you to seek the common ground between you.
- Summaries help you to move beyond adversarial thinking.

Simple summaries are useful at key turning points in a conversation. At the start, summarise your most important point or your objective. As you want to move on from one stage to the next, summarise where you think you have both got to and check that the other person agrees with you. At the end of the conversation, summarise what you have achieved and the action steps you both need to take.

To summarise means to reinterpret the other person's ideas in your own language. It involves *recognising* the specific point they've made, *appreciating* the position from which they say it and *understanding* the beliefs that inform that position. Recognising what someone says doesn't imply that you agree with it. Rather, it implies that you have taken the point into account. Appreciating the other person's feelings on the matter doesn't mean that you feel the same way, but it does show that you respect those feelings. And understanding the belief may not mean that you share it, but it does mean that you consider it important. Shared problem-solving becomes much easier if those three basic summarising tactics come into play.

Of course, summaries must be genuine. They must be supported by all the non-verbal cues that demonstrate your recognition, appreciation and understanding. And those cues will look more genuine if you actually recognise, appreciate and – at least seek to – understand.

use visuals

It's said that people remember about 20 per cent of what they hear, and over 80 per cent of what they see. If communication is the process of making your thinking visible, your conversations will certainly benefit from some way of being able to *see* your ideas.

There are lots of ways in which you can achieve a visual image of your conversation. The obvious ways include scribbling on the nearest bit of paper or using a flip chart. Less obvious visual aids include the gestures and facial expressions you make. Less obvious still – but possibly the most powerful – are word pictures: the images people can create in each other's minds with the words they use.

recording your ideas on paper

In my experience, conversations nearly always benefit from being recorded visually. The patterns and pictures and diagrams and doodles that you scribble on a pad help you to listen, to summarise and to keep track of what you've covered. More creatively, they become the *focus* for the conversation: in making the shape of your thinking visible on the page, you can ensure that you are indeed sharing understanding.

Recording ideas in this way – on a pad or a flip chart – also helps to make conversations more democratic. Once on paper, ideas become common property: all parties to the conversation can see them, add to them, comment on them and combine them.

What is really needed, of course, is a technique that is flexible enough to follow the conversation wherever it might go: a technique that can accommodate diverse ideas while maintaining your focus on a clear objective. If the technique could actually help you to develop new ideas, so much the better.

Fortunately, such a technique exists. It's called mindmapping. Mindmaps are powerful first-stage thinking tools. By emphasising the links between ideas, they encourage you to think more creatively and efficiently.

To make a mindmap:

- Put a visual image of your subject in the centre of a plain piece of paper.
- Write down anything that comes to mind that connects to the central idea.
- Write single words, in BLOCK CAPITALS, along lines radiating from the centre.
- Main ideas will tend to gravitate to the centre of the map; details will radiate towards the edge.
- Every line must connect to at least one other line.
- Use visual display: colour, pattern, highlights.
- Identify the groups of ideas that you have created. If you wish, give each a heading and put the groups into numerical order.

Mindmaps are incredibly versatile conversational tools. They can help you in any situation where you need to record, assemble, organise or generate ideas. They force you to listen attentively, so that you can make meaningful connections; they help you to concentrate on what you are saying, rather than writing; and they store complicated information on one sheet of paper.

Try out mindmaps in relatively simple conversations to begin with. Record a phone conversation using a mindmap and see how well you get on with the technique. Extend your practice to face-to-face conversations and invite the other person to look at and contribute to the map.

A variation on mindmaps is to use sticky notes to record ideas. By placing one idea on each note, you can assemble the notes on a wall or tabletop and move them around to find logical connections or associations between them. This technique is particularly useful in brainstorming sessions or conversations that are seeking to solve complex problems.

using metaphors

Metaphors are images of ideas in concrete form. The word means 'transferring' or 'carrying over'. A metaphor carries your meaning from one thing to another. It enables your listener to *see* something in a new way, by picturing it as something else. Metaphors use the imagination to support and develop your ideas.

Metaphors bring your meaning alive in the listener's mind. They narrow the listener's focus and direct their attention to what the speaker wants them to see. They stir their feelings. Metaphors can build your commitment to another person's ideas and help you to remember them.

If you want to find a metaphor to make your thinking more creative and your conversation more interesting, you might start by simply listening out for them in the conversation you are holding. You will find you use many metaphors without even noticing them. If you are still looking, you might try asking yourself some simple questions:

- ■ What's the problem like?
- ■ If this were a different situation – a game of cricket, a medieval castle, a mission to Mars, a kindergarten – how would I deal with it?
- ■ How would a different kind of person manage the issue: a gardener, a politician, an engineer, a hairdresser, an actor?

- What does this situation *feel* like?
- If this problem were an animal, what species of animal would it be?
- How could I describe what's going on as if it were in the human body?

Explore your answers to these questions and develop the images that spring to mind. You need to be in a calm, receptive frame of mind to do this: the conversation needs to slow down and reflect on its own progress. Finding metaphors is very much first-stage thinking, because metaphors are tools to help you see reality in new ways.

You will know when you've hit on a productive metaphor. The conversation will suddenly catch fire (that's a metaphor!). You will feel a sudden injection of energy and excitement as you realise that you are thinking in a completely new way.

the skills of enquiry

The skills of enquiry are the skills of listening. And the quality of your conversation depends on the quality of your listening.

Only by enquiring into the other person's ideas can you respond honestly and fully to them. Only by discovering the mental models and beliefs that underlie those ideas can you explore the landscape of their thinking. Only by finding out how they think can you begin to persuade them to your way of thinking.

Skilled enquiry actually helps the other person to think better. Listening – real, deep, attentive listening – can liberate their thinking.

I've summarised the skills of enquiry under six headings:

- paying attention;
- treating the speaker as an equal;
- cultivating ease;
- encouraging;
- asking quality questions;
- rationing information.

Acquiring these skills will help you to give the other person the respect and space they deserve to develop their own ideas – to make their thinking visible.

paying attention

Paying attention means concentrating on what the other person is saying. That sounds simple: how can you listen without paying attention?

Of course, this is what happens most of the time. You think you're listening, but you aren't. You finish the other person's sentences. You interrupt. You moan, sigh, grunt, laugh or cough. You fill pauses with your own thoughts, stories or theories. You look at your watch or around the room. You think about the next meeting, or the next report, or the next meal. You frown, tap your fingers, destroy paperclips and glance at your diary. You give advice. You give more advice.

You think your own thoughts when you should be silencing them. Real listening means shutting down your own thinking and allowing the other person's thinking to enter.

A lot of what you hear when you listen to another person is your effect on them. If you are paying proper attention, they will become more intelligent and articulate. Poor attention will make them hesitate, stumble and doubt the soundness of their thinking. Poor attention makes people more stupid.

I think that, deep down, we have two mental models about listening. We hold them so deeply that we're hardly aware of them. And they do more to damage the quality of our listening than anything else.

The first mental model is that *people listen in order to work out a reply*. This seems a reasonable enough idea. But it's wrong. If people listen so that they can work out what *they* should think, then they aren't listening closely enough to what *the other person* thinks. They are not paying attention.

The second mental model is that *people reply in order to tell the other person what to think*. In fact, this model implies that people only talk to other people because they *want* their own ideas. This model, too, is wrong.

Listening well means helping the other person to find out their ideas. The mind containing the problem probably also contains the solution. Their solution is likely to be much better *because it's theirs*. Paying attention means helping the other person to make their thinking visible.

Of course, the other person may actually want advice. But don't assume that this is the case. Wait for them to ask; if necessary, ask them what they want from you. Don't rush. Give them the chance to find their own ideas first. Paying attention in this way will probably slow the conversation down more than you feel is comfortable. Adjust your own tempo to that of the other person. Wait longer than you want to.

Listen. Listen. And then listen some more. And when they can't think of anything else to say, ask: 'What else do you think about this? What else can you think of? What else comes to mind?'. That invitation to talk more can bring even the weariest brain back to life.

interrupting

Interrupting is the most obvious symptom of poor attention. It's irresistible. Some demon inside us seems to compel us to fill the other person's pauses with words. It's as if the very idea of silence is terrifying.

Mostly people interrupt because they are making assumptions. Here are a few. Next time you interrupt someone in a conversation, ask yourself which of them you are applying.

▓ My idea is better than theirs.
▓ The answer is more important than the problem.
▓ I have to utter my idea fast and if I don't interrupt, I'll lose my chance (or forget it).
▓ I know what they're going to say.
▓ They don't need to finish the sentence because my rewrite is an improvement.
▓ They can't improve this idea any further, so I might as well improve it for them.

▓ I'm more important than they are.
▓ It's more important for me to be seen to have a good idea than for me to let them finish.
▓ Interrupting will save time.

Put like that, these assumptions are shown up for what they are: presumptuous, arrogant, silly. You're usually wrong when you assume that you know what the other person is about to say. If you allow them to continue, they will often come up with something more interesting, more colourful and more personal.

allowing quiet

Once you stop interrupting, the conversation will become quieter. Pauses will appear. The other person will stop talking and you won't fill the silence.

These pauses are like junctions. The conversation has come to a crossroads. You have a number of choices about where you might go next. Either of you might make that choice. If you are interested in persuading, you will seize the opportunity and make the choice yourself. But, if you are enquiring, then you give the speaker the privilege of making the choice.

There are two kinds of pause. One is a filled pause; the other is empty. Learn to distinguish between the two.

Some pauses are filled with thought. Sometimes, the speaker will stop. They will go quiet, perhaps suddenly. They will look elsewhere, probably into a longer distance. They are busy on an excursion. You're not invited. But they will want you to be there at the crossroads when they come back. You are privileged that they have trusted you to wait. So wait.

The other kind of pause is an empty one. Nothing much is happening. The speaker doesn't stop suddenly; instead, they seem to fade away. You are standing at the crossroads in the conversation together, and neither of you is moving. The energy seems to drop out of the conversation. The speaker's eyes don't focus anywhere. If they are comfortable in your company, they may focus on you as a cue for you to choose what move to make.

Wait out the pause. If the pause is empty, the speaker will probably say so in a few moments. 'I can't think of anything else.' 'That's it, really.' 'So. There we are. I'm stuck now.' Try asking that question: 'Can you think of anything else?' Resist the temptation to move the conversation on by asking a more specific question. The moment you do that, you have closed down every other possible journey that you might take together: you are dictating the road to travel. Make sure that you only do so once the other person is ready to let you take the lead.

showing that you are paying attention

Your face will show the other person whether you are paying attention to them. In particular, your eyes will speak volumes about the quality of your listening.

By behaving *as if* you are interested, you can sometimes *become* more interested. Discipline yourself to use an expression that tells the other person that they matter to you, that you are interested in what they're saying and that you are not in a rush. Try not to frown or tighten your facial muscles. Remember, too, that a rigid smile can be just as off-putting as a perpetual scowl. In the end, your face won't look interested unless you *are* interested.

Keep your eyes on the person doing the talking. The speaker will probably look away frequently: that's what people do when they're thinking. It helps if you are in relative positions where they can do that easily. Sitting at an angle of about 60 degrees, for example, gives the other person's eyes a useful escape lane. But you should look at them, and keep looking.

It may be that such attentive looking actually inhibits the speaker. In some cultures, looking equates to staring and is a sign of disrespect. You need to be sensitive to these possible

individual or cultural distinctions and adapt your eye movements accordingly. Generally, people do not look nearly
enough at those they are listening to. The person speaking will
pick up the quality of your attention through your eyes –
possibly unconsciously – and the quality of their thinking will
improve as a result.

treating the speaker as an equal

You will only be able to enquire well if you treat the speaker as
an equal. The moment you make your relationship unequal,
confusion will result. If you place yourself higher than them in
status, you will discourage them from thinking well. If you
place them higher than you, you will start to allow your own
inhibitions to disrupt your attention to what they are saying.

Patronising the speaker is the greatest enemy of equality in
conversations. This conversational sin derives from the way
people are treated as children – and the way some people
subsequently treat children. Sometimes children have to be
treated like children. It is necessary to:

- decide for them;
- direct them;
- tell them what to do;
- assume that adults know better than they do;
- worry about them;
- take care of them;
- control them;
- think for them.

There is a tendency to carry this patronising behaviour over
into conversations with other adults. As soon as you think you
know better than the other person, or provide the answers for
them, or suggest that their thinking is inadequate, you are
patronising them. It can be subtle: patronising behaviour often

covers itself in the guise of being caring or supportive. But it stops people thinking for themselves. It slows down their thinking and makes them less intelligent. You can't patronise somebody and pay them close attention at the same time.

Treat the other person as an equal and you won't be able to patronise them. If you don't value somebody's ideas, don't hold conversations with them. But if you want ideas that are better than your own, if you want better outcomes and improved working relationships, work hard on giving other people the respect that they and their ideas deserve.

cultivating ease

Good thinking happens in a relaxed environment. Cultivating ease will allow you to enquire more deeply, and discover more ideas.

Most people aren't used to ease and may actually argue against it. They're so used to urgency that they can't imagine working in any other way. Many organisations actually dispel ease from the workplace. Ease is equated with sloth. If you're not working flat out, chased by deadlines and juggling 50 assignments at the same time, you're not worth your salary. Urgency is cultivated. It is assumed that the best thinking happens in such a climate.

This is wrong. Urgency keeps people from thinking well. They're too busy doing. After all, doing is what gets results, isn't it? Not when people have to think to get them. Sometimes, the best results only appear by *not* doing: by paying attention to someone else's ideas with a mind that is alert, comfortable, and at ease. When you are at ease, the solution to a problem will appear as if by magic.

Find the time for conversation. If the situation is urgent, postpone conversations. If you must hold a conversation, make a space for it and cultivate ease. Be realistic about the amount of time available, and think about how you will use that time well. Banish distractions. Unplug and turn off the phones. Leave the building. Barricade the door. Make space. The curious thing is that once you banish urgency, you seem actually to create time. You will find you experience time differently when you are at ease. And you will achieve more.

Cultivating ease in a conversation is largely a behavioural skill. Make yourself comfortable. Lean back, breathe out, smile, look keen, and slow down your speaking rhythm.

encouraging

In order to liberate the other person's ideas, you may need to do more than pay attention, treat them as an equal and cultivate ease. You may need to actively encourage them to give you their ideas.

All sorts of factors may be inhibiting someone from speaking honestly and openly. Think back to our earlier exploration of the factors that affect conversations: context, relationship, structure, behaviour. The other person may be coming into the conversation from a situation that you hardly understand. They may be in awe of you or lack respect for you, or be suspicious about your own motives for holding the conversation. Your behaviour may create a discouraging impression from the start of the conversation.

Remember that the other person's thinking is to a large extent the result of the effect you have on them. So if you:

■ suggest that they change the subject,
■ try to convince them of your point of view before listening to their point of view,
■ reply tit-for-tat to their remarks, or
■ encourage them to compete with you,

you aren't encouraging them to develop their thinking. You're not enquiring properly.

Competitiveness is one of the worst enemies of encouragement. It's easy to slip into a ritual of using the speaker's ideas to promote your own. It's all part of the tradition of adversarial thinking that is so highly valued in Western society.

If the speaker feels that you are competing with them in the conversation, they will limit not only what they say but also what they think. Competition forces people to think only those thoughts that will help them win. Similarly, if you feel that the speaker is trying to compete with you, don't allow yourself to enter the competition. This is much harder to achieve. The Ladder of Inference (see Chapter 3) is one very powerful tool that will help you to defuse competitiveness in your conversations.

Instead of competing, welcome the difference in your points of view. Encourage a positive acknowledgement that you see things differently and that you must deal with that difference if the conversation is to move forward.

asking quality questions

Questions are the most obvious way to enquire into other people's thinking. Yet it's astonishing how rarely managers ask quality questions.

Questions, of course, can be loaded with assumptions. They can be politically charged. In some conversations, the most important questions are never asked because to do so would be to challenge the centre of authority. To ask a question can sometimes seem like revealing an unacceptable ignorance. In some organisations, to ask them is simply 'not done'. 'Questioning', said Samuel Johnson on one occasion, 'is not the mode of conversation among gentlemen.'

Questions can also be used in ways that don't promote enquiry. Specifically, managers sometimes use questions to:

- ▓ emphasise the difference between their ideas and other people's;
- ▓ ridicule or make the other person look foolish;
- ▓ criticise in disguise;
- ▓ find fault;
- ▓ make themselves look clever;
- ▓ express a point of view in code;
- ▓ force the other person into a corner;
- ▓ create an argument.

The only legitimate use of a question is to foster enquiry. Questions help you to:

- ▓ find out facts;
- ▓ check your understanding;
- ▓ help the other person to improve their understanding;
- ▓ invite the other person to examine your own thinking;
- ▓ request action.

The best questions open up the other person's thinking. A question that helps the other person think further, develop an idea or make their thoughts more visible to you both, is a high-quality question.

It is important to become more confident in asking the important questions. If you want to enquire more fully in your conversations, you need to think about why you ask questions, how you ask them and what kinds of questions you can use.

A whole repertoire of questions is available to help you enquire more fully. Specifically, six types of question can be considered:

- ▓ **Closed questions.** Can only be answered 'yes' or 'no'.
- ▓ **Leading questions.** Put the answer into the other person's mouth.
- ▓ **Controlling questions.** Help you to take the lead in the conversation.

■ **Probing questions.** Build on an earlier question, or dig deeper.

■ **Open questions.** Cannot be answered 'yes' or 'no'.

■ **Reflecting questions.** Restate the last remark with no new request.

Remember also the Ladder of Inference from Chapter 3. This powerful tool can provide questions that allow you to enquire into the speaker's thinking. You can also use it to invite them to enquire into yours.

The highest quality questions actually liberate the other person's thinking. They remove the assumptions that block thinking and replace them with other assumptions that set it free. The key is identifying the assumption that might be limiting the other person's thinking. You don't have to guess aright: asking the question may tell you whether you've identified it correctly; if it doesn't, it may well open up the speaker's thinking anyway.

These high quality questions are broadly 'What if' questions. You can either ask a question in the form 'What if this assumption weren't true?' or in the form 'What if the opposite assumption were true?'.

Examples of the first kind of question might include:

■ What if you became chief executive tomorrow?

■ What if I weren't your manager?

■ What if you weren't limited in your use of equipment?

Examples of the second kind might include:

■ What if you weren't limited by a budget?

■ What if customers were actually flocking to us?

■ What if you knew that you were vital to the company's success?

People are often inhibited from developing their thinking by two deep assumptions. One is that they are incapable of thinking well about something, or achieving something. The other is that they don't deserve to think well or achieve. Asking good questions can help you to encourage the other person to overcome these inhibitors and grow as a competent thinker.

rationing information

Information is power. Sometimes, as part of enquiry, you can supply information that will empower the speaker to think better. Withholding information is an abuse of your power over them.

The difficulty is that giving information disrupts the dynamic of listening and enquiring. A few simple guidelines will help you to ration the information that you supply:

- ■ **Don't interrupt.** Let the speaker finish before giving any new information. Don't force information into the middle of their sentence.
- ■ **Time your intervention.** Ask yourself when the most appropriate time might be to offer the information.
- ■ **Filter the information.** Only offer information that you think will improve the speaker's thinking. Resist the temptation to amplify some piece of information that is not central to the direction of their thinking.
- ■ **Don't give information to show off.** You may be tempted to give information to demonstrate how expert or up to date you are. Resist that temptation.

Asking the speaker for information is also something you should ration carefully. You need to make that request at the right time, and for the right reason. To ask for it at the wrong time may close down their thinking and deny you a whole area of valuable ideas.

Following this advice may mean that you have to listen without fully understanding what the speaker is saying. You may even completely misunderstand for a while. Remember that enquiry is about helping the other person clarify their thinking. If asking for information will help only you – and not the speaker – you should consider delaying your request. In enquiry, it's more important to let the speaker do their thinking than to understand fully what they are saying. This may seem strange. But if you let the speaker work out their thinking rather than keeping you fully informed, they will probably be better able to summarise their ideas clearly to you when they've finished.

the skills of persuasion

The ability to persuade and influence has never been in more demand among managers. The days of simply telling people what to do and expecting them to do it are long gone. Now you have to be able to 'sell your ideas'.

The key to effective persuasion is having powerful ideas and delivering them well. Ideas are the currency of communication. Information alone will never influence anyone to act. Only ideas have the power to persuade.

The old word for this is rhetoric. Since ancient times, the art of rhetoric has taught people how to assemble and deliver their ideas. Few people – at least in Europe – now study rhetoric systematically. Yet, by applying a few simple principles, you can radically improve the quality of your persuasion.

character, logic and passion

Aristotle, the grandfather of rhetoric, claimed that it is possible to persuade in two ways: through the evidence brought to support a case; and through what he called 'artistic' persuasion.

Evidence might consist of documents or witnesses: you might use spreadsheets and experts to give the direct evidence to support a case. 'Artistic' persuasion combines three internal traits in you, as the persuader:

- your character or reputation;
- the quality of your logic;
- the passion that you bring to your argument.

You might say that effective persuasion means communicating equally with your heart, your head and your soul.

character

Character (or *ethos*) is shorthand for the integrity and authority that you transmit to your audience. Why should your listener believe what you are telling them? What are your qualifications for saying all this? Where is your experience and expertise? How does your reputation stand with them? What value can you add to the argument from your own experience? Your character creates the trust upon which you can build your argument.

logic

Logic is the work of rational thought. Reasoning is the method by which you assemble your ideas (the Greeks called it *logos*). Logic comes in two forms:

- **Deductive logic** assembles ideas in a sequence. It begins with an idea, adds a second idea that comments on the first, and draws a conclusion that is the third idea. A classic example of deductive logic is: 'Socrates is a man. All men are mortal. Therefore, Socrates is mortal.' A more commercial example might be: 'You are looking to invest in companies with high rates of growth. Company A has a high rate of growth. Therefore, you should invest in Company A.'

■ **Inductive logic** assembles ideas in a pyramid. It groups ideas together and then summarises them with a governing idea. A simple example might be:

We have found three companies that meet your criteria for investment.

1. Company A meets the criteria.
2. Company B meets the criteria.
3. Company C meets the criteria.

passion

Passion (or *pathos*) is the commitment and feeling that you bring to your subject. If you aren't fired up by the idea, you can't expect others to be. Many organisational cultures distrust passion, though many of the people working in them respond positively to any outside injection of passion into their work. To show passion may not be 'the done thing'. Yet, without passion, nothing is ever achieved. The great inventors, artists and entrepreneurs are distinguished not merely by their talent, but also by the burning conviction that drove them to achieve, often against great odds.

You can't fake passion. If you want to persuade someone of the power of an idea, you must feel that power in your soul. This may not be easy. After all, not every idea is worth a great deal of passion. But if you want to do a good job, if you want to make your contribution, if you care about the future of your organisation, then passion is probably not far away.

All three of these qualities – character, reasoning and passion – must be present if you want to persuade someone. The *process* of working out how to persuade them consists of five key elements:

- identifying the core idea;
- arranging your ideas logically;
- developing an appropriate style in the language you use;
- remembering your ideas;
- delivering your ideas with words, visual cues and non-verbal behaviour.

what's the big idea?

If you want to persuade someone, you must have a message. What do you want to say? What's the big idea? You must know what idea you want to promote. A single governing idea is more likely to persuade your listener than a group of ideas, simply because one strong idea is easier to remember. We work in a world of too much information and too few ideas. Without a driving idea, you will never be able to persuade anyone to believe or do anything.

Begin by gathering ideas. Conduct imaginary conversations in your head and note down the kind of things you might say. Capture ideas as they occur to you and store them on a pad or in a file. Spend as much time as you can on this activity before the conversation itself.

Having captured and stored some ideas, ask three fundamental questions:

- 'What is my objective?' What do I want to achieve? What would I like to see happen?
- 'Who am I talking to?' Why am I talking to this person about this objective? What do they already know? What more do they need to know? What do I want them to *do*? What kind of ideas will be most likely to convince them?
- 'What is the most important thing I have to say to them?' If I were only allowed a few minutes with them,

what would I say to convince them – or, at least, to persuade them to keep listening?

Think hard about these three questions. Imagine that you had only a few *seconds* to get your message across. What would you say?

Try to create a single sentence. Remember that you can't express an idea without uttering a sentence. Above all, this idea should be *new* to the listener. After all, there's no point in trying to persuade them of something they already know or agree with!

Once you have decided on your message, you must consider whether you think it is appropriate both to your objective and to your listener. Does this sentence express what you want to achieve? Is it in language that the listener will understand easily? Is it simple enough? This is a problem particularly when managers who are technical specialists try to persuade more senior managers whose expertise is more general. The jargon and detail get in the way of the key message that the persuading manager needs to put across.

Now test your message sentence. If you were to speak this sentence to your listener, would they ask you a question? If so, what would that question be? If your message is a clear one, it will provoke *one* of these three questions:

■ 'Why?'
■ 'How?'
■ 'Which ones?'

If you can't imagine your listener asking any of these questions, they're unlikely to be interested in your message. So try another. If you can imagine them asking more than one of these questions, try to simplify your message.

Now work out how to bring your listener to the place where they will accept this message. You must 'bring them around to your way of thinking'. This means starting where the listener is standing and gently guiding them to where you want them to be. Once you are standing in the same place, there is a much stronger chance that you will see things the same way. Persuading them will become a great deal easier.

People will only be persuaded by ideas that interest them. Your listener will only be interested in your message because it answers some need or question that already exists in their mind. An essential element in delivering your message, then, is demonstrating that it relates to that need or that question.

Here is a simple four-point structure that will bring your listener to the point where they can accept your message. I remember it by using the letters SPQR.

situation

Briefly tell the listener something they already know. Make a statement about the matter that you *know* they will agree with. This demonstrates that you are on their territory: you understand their situation and can appreciate their point of view. Try to state the Situation in such a way that the listener expects to hear more. Think of this as a kind of 'Once upon a time...'. It's an opener, a scene-setting statement that prepares them for what's to come.

problem

Now identify a Problem that has arisen within the Situation. The listener may know about the Problem; they may not. But they certainly *should* know about it! In other words, the Problem should be *their* problem at least as much as yours.

Problems, of course, come in many shapes and sizes. It's important that you identify a Problem that the listener will recognise. It must clearly relate to the Situation that you have set up: it poses a threat to it or creates a challenge within it.

---

what's the problem?

Situation	Problem
Stable, agreed status quo	Something's gone wrong
	Something could go wrong
	Something's changed
	Something could change
	Something new has arisen
	Someone has a different point of view
	We don't know what to do
	There are a number of things we could do

Problems can be positive as well as negative. You may want to alert your listener to an opportunity that has arisen within the Situation.

question

The Problem causes the listener to ask a Question (or would do so, if they were aware of it). Once again, the listener may or may not be asking the Question. If they are, you are better placed to be able to answer it. If they are not, you may have to carefully get them to agree that this Question is worth asking.

---

what's the question?

Situation	Problem	Question
Stable, agreed status quo	Something's gone wrong	What do we do?
	Something could go wrong	How do we stop it?
	Something's changed	How do we adjust to it?
	Something could change	How do we prepare for it?

Something new has arisen	What can we do?
Someone has a different point of view	Who's right?
We don't know what to do	What do we do? or How do we choose?
There are a number of things we could do	Which course do we take?

response

Your Response or answer to the Question is your message. In other words, the message should naturally emerge as the logical and powerful answer to the Question raised in the listener's mind by the Problem!

This is a classic story-telling framework. It is also well known as a method management consultants use in the introductions to their proposals. Your aim in using it is to guide the listener from where they are to where you want them to be: to prepare them for your message and the ideas that support it. The trick is to take your listener through the four stages *quickly*. Don't be tempted to fill out the story with lots of detail. As you use SPQR, remember these three key points:

1. SPQR should remind the listener rather than persuade them. Until you get to the message, you shouldn't include any idea that you would need to prove.
2. Think of SPQR as a story. Keep it moving. Keep the listener's interest.
3. Adapt the stages of the story to the needs of the listener. Make sure that they agree to the first three stages without difficulty. Make sure that you are addressing their needs, values, priorities. Put everything in their terms.

arranging your ideas

Logic is the method by which you assemble ideas into a coherent structure. It's the logic that makes the structure of your ideas persuasive. So you must have a number of key ideas that support the message you have chosen. Ideally, they are answers to the question you can imagine your listener asking when you utter your message.

---

finding your key ideas

If your message provokes the listener to ask:	Your key ideas will be:
'Why?'	Reasons, benefits or causes
'How?'	Methods, ways to do something, procedures
'Which ones?'	These ones: items in a list

There are two ways to organise ideas logically. They can be organised deductively, in a sequence, and inductively, in a pyramid.

arguing deductively

Deductive logic takes the form of a syllogism: an argument in which a conclusion is inferred from two statements. To argue deductively:

- ■ make a statement;
- ■ make a second statement that relates to the first – by commenting on either the subject of the first statement, or on what you have said about that subject;
- ■ state the implication of these two statements being true simultaneously. This conclusion is your message.

arguing inductively

Inductive logic works by stating a governing idea and then delivering a group of other ideas that the governing idea summarises. Another name for this kind of logic is *grouping and summarising*.

Inductive logic creates pyramids of ideas. You can test the logic of the structure by asking whether the ideas in any one group are answers to the question that the summarising idea provokes. (You've done this already when formulating your message.) That question will be one of three: 'Why?', 'How?' or 'Which ones?'.

Inductive logic tends to be more powerful in business than deductive logic. Deductive logic brings two major risks with it:

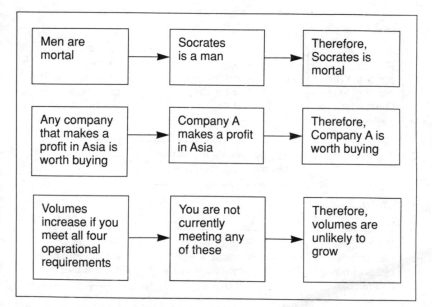

Figure 5.1   *Some examples of deductive reasoning*

1. It demands real patience on the part of the listener. If you put too many ideas into your sequence, you may stretch their patience to breaking point.
2. You may undermine your own argument. Each stage in the deductive sequence is an invitation to the listener to disagree. And they only have to disagree with one of the stages for the whole sequence to collapse.

Inductive logic avoids both of these perils. First, it doesn't strain the listener's patience so much because the main idea – the message – appears at the beginning. Secondly, a pyramid is

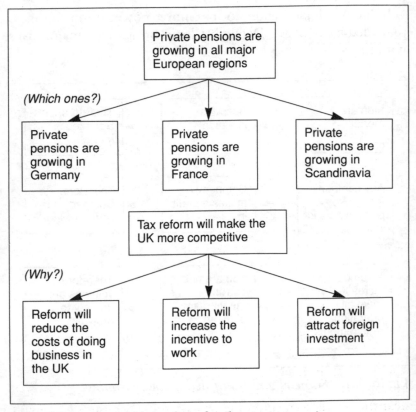

Figure 5.2 *Some examples of inductive reasoning*

less likely to collapse than a strung-out sequence of ideas. It's easier to construct than a deductive sequence because you can see more clearly whether your other ideas support your message. And the message has a good chance of surviving even if one of the supporting ideas is removed. Pyramids of ideas satisfy our thirst for answers now and evidence later. They allow you to be more creative in assembling your ideas and they put the message right at the front.

Deductive logic is only really useful for establishing whether something is *true*. Inductive logic can also help you to establish whether something is *worth doing*.

expressing your ideas

It's not enough to have coherent ideas, logically organised. You have to bring the ideas alive in the listener's mind. You have to use words to create pictures and feelings that will stimulate their senses as well as their brain.

People don't remember words. They forget nearly everything others say. But they *do* remember images – particularly images that excite sensory impressions and feelings. So, if you want your ideas to stick, you must stamp them in the listener's mind in some non-verbal form. If you can excite their imagination through the senses and stimulate some feeling in them, you will be able to plant the accompanying idea in their long-term memory.

Memory = image + feeling

The word 'image', of course, powerfully suggests something visual. But you can create *impressions* through any of the five senses: sight, hearing, touch, smell and taste. Some people will be convinced by pictures; others will only be persuaded if they hear the words come out of their own mouth. Others again will only remember and learn by touching: they are the 'hands-on' people who demand demonstrations and practice.

Neuro-linguistic programming (NLP) works on the basis of people's natural sensory preferences for receiving information. Some people are visually oriented, others auditory, and a third group kinaesthetic (they are the 'hands-on' ones). You may be able to guess something of your listener's own style through the language they use: 'I see what you mean', for example, or 'I hear what you're saying', or maybe 'This idea just doesn't feel right'. NLP seeks to develop this awareness of sensory preference into a systematic approach to communicating.

Even without training or study, however, you can become more attuned to the way you respond to ideas with your senses. Whenever you are seeking to persuade someone with an idea, think about how each of the five senses might respond to it. Try to create an impression of the idea that will appeal to one or other of the senses. You'll find that the idea comes magically alive.

examples

Perhaps the simplest way to bring an idea alive is to offer a concrete example. Find an instance where the idea has been put into practice, or where it has created real results – either useful or disastrous.

Examples can be powerfully and immediately persuasive. Once we know that something definite has happened to demonstrate the validity of an idea, we will take the idea itself a lot more seriously. Many managers seem hesitant to use concrete examples. Perhaps they sense that simple examples may trivialise their ideas, or that talking in bold abstractions is more impressive. It's certainly easier to befuddle and confuse your listener by talking in abstract terms; but a single clear example will bring your idea alive and make it stick in your listener's mind in a way that dozens of long words would never do.

stories

Stories are special kinds of examples. They lend weight to the example by making it personal. They also have the benefit of entertaining the listener, keeping them in suspense and releasing an emotional response with a surprising revelation. Much everyday persuasion and explanation is in the form of stories: gossip, jokes, speculation, 'war stories' or plain rumour.

Stories work best when they are concrete and personal. Tell your own, authentic stories. They will display your character and your passion. They will also be easier to remember! If you want to tell another person's story, explain that it's not yours and tell it swiftly. A story will persuade your listener if it has a clear point. Without a point, it can become counterproductive: an annoying diversion and a waste of time. You may need to make it clear: 'and the point of the story is...'.

using metaphors

Using metaphors, as discussed in Chapter 3, is the technique of expressing one thing in terms of another. Metaphors allow you to see things in new ways by showing how they relate to others. The most persuasive metaphors are those that make a direct appeal to the senses and to experience.

Metaphors create meaning. They burn ideas into your listener's mind (that's a metaphor!). They help listeners to remember by creating pictures (or sounds, or tastes, or smells) that they can store in their mind (I'm using the metaphor of a cupboard or library to explain some part of the mind's working.)

remembering your ideas

Memory played a vital role in the art of rhetoric in the days before printing. With no ready means of making notes or easy access to books, remembering ideas and their relationships was an essential skill. Whole systems of memory were invented to help people store information and recall it at will.

These days, memory hardly seems to figure as a life skill – except for passing examinations. It seems that technology has taken its place. There is no *need* to remember: merely to read and store e-mails, pick up messages (voice and text) on the mobile, plug in, surf and download...

If you can't begin to persuade someone without a heap of spreadsheets and a briefcase full of project designs to refer to, don't start. Nobody was ever persuaded by watching someone recite from a sheaf of notes.

Find a way to bring the ideas off paper and into your head. Give yourself some clear mental signposts so that you can find your way from one idea to the next. Write a few notes on a card or on the back of your hand. Draw a mindmap. Make it colourful. If you've assembled a mental pyramid, draw it on a piece of paper and carry it with you. Have some means available to draw your thoughts as you explain them: a notepad, a flip chart, a white board. Invite the other person to join in: encourage them to think of this as the shape of *their* thinking.

delivering effectively

Delivery means supporting your ideas with effective behaviour. Chapter 2 showed how non-verbal communication is a vital component in creating understanding. When you are seeking to persuade, your behaviour will be the most persuasive thing about you. If you are saying one thing but your body is saying another, no one will believe your words.

Think about the style of delivery your listener might prefer. Do they favour a relaxed, informal conversational style or a more formal, presentational delivery? Are they interested in the broad picture or do they want lots of supporting detail? Will they want to ask questions?

Delivery is broadly about three kinds of activity. Think about the way you use your:

- eyes;
- voice;
- body.

effective eye contact

People speak more with their eyes than with their voice. Maintain eye contact with your listener. If you are talking to more than one person, include everybody with your eyes. Focus on their eyes: don't look through them. There are two occasions when you might break eye contact: when you are thinking about what to say next; and when you are looking at notes, a mindmap or some other object of common attention.

using your voice

Your voice will sound more persuasive if it is not too high, too fast or too thin. Work to regulate and strengthen your breathing while you speak. Breathe deep and slow. Let your voice emerge more from your body than from your throat. Slow down the pace of your voice, too: it can be all too easy to gabble when you are involved in an argument or nervous about the other person's reactions. The more body your voice has, and the more measured your vocal delivery, the more convincing you will sound.

persuasive body language

Your face, your limbs and your body posture will all contribute to the total effect your ideas have on the listener. To start with, try not to frown. Keep your facial muscles moving and pay attention to keeping your neck muscles relaxed. Use your hands to paint pictures, to help you find the right words and express yourself fully.

Professional persuaders observe their listeners' behaviour and quietly mirror it. If you are relaxed with the other person, such mirroring will tend to happen naturally: you may find you are crossing your legs in similar ways or moving your arms in roughly the same way. Try consciously to adapt your own posture and movement to that of the person listening to you. Do more: take the lead. Don't sit back or close your body off when you are seeking to persuade; bring yourself forward, open yourself up and present yourself along with your ideas.

interviews: holding a formal conversation

Every manager holds interviews. To be able to hold a structured interview with someone to achieve a clear goal is a fundamental managerial skill.

Interviews tend to make people nervous. And it's not only the interviewee who becomes anxious at the thought of being questioned (or interrogated, or grilled, or examined...); interviewers also frequently admit to being terrified at the prospect of having to conduct an interview.

when is an interview not an interview?

The word 'interview' simply means 'looking between us': an interview is an exchange of views. Any conversation – conducted well – is such an exchange. Interviews differ from other conversations in that they:

- ■ are held for a very specific reason;
- ■ aim at a particular outcome;
- ■ are more carefully and consciously structured;
- ■ must usually cover predetermined matters of concern;
- ■ are called and led by one person – the interviewer;
- ■ are usually recorded.

This chapter will look at the following four types of interview:

- ■ appraisal;
- ■ delegation;
- ■ coaching;
- ■ counselling.

Each type of interview will demand a range of skills from you, the interviewer. All of the skills of enquiry and persuasion that have been explored so far in this book will come into play at some point.

preparing for the interview

Prepare for the interview by considering three questions:

- ■ What's my objective?
- ■ What do I need?
- ■ When and where?

what's my objective?

What do you want to achieve in the interview? You must decide, for you are calling the interview. Do you want to discipline a member of staff for risking an accident, or influence their attitude to safety? Are you trying to offload a boring routine task or seeking to delegate as a way of developing a member of your team? Are you counselling or coaching?

Setting a clear objective is the only way you will be able to measure the interview's success. And it is essential if you want to be able to decide on the style and structure of the interview.

what do I need?

Think about the information you will need before and during the interview. Think also about what information the interviewee will need. What are the key areas you need to cover? In what order? What questions do you need to ask?

You may also need other kinds of equipment to help you: notepads, flip charts, files, samples of material or machinery. You may even need a witness to ensure that the interview is seen to be conducted professionally and fairly.

when and where?

When do you propose to interview? For how long? The time of day is as important as the day you choose. Certain times of day are notoriously difficult for interview: after lunch, for example – or *during* lunch! Remember also that an interview that goes on too long will become counterproductive.

The quality of the interview will be strongly influenced by its venue. You may decide that your office is too formal or intimidating; on the other hand, interviewing in a crowded public area or in the pub can offend the sense of privacy that any interview should encourage. You may decide to conduct some parts of an interview in different places.

Think also about the climate you set up for the interviewee. Sitting them on a low chair, beyond a desk, facing a sunny window, with nowhere to put a cup of coffee, will obviously set up an unpleasant atmosphere.

structuring the interview

Interviews, like other conversations, naturally fall into a structure. Interviewers sometimes try to press an interview forward towards a result without allowing enough time for the early stages.

Every interview can be structured using the WASP structure that was examined in Chapter 3. This structure reinforces the fact that both stages of thinking are important.

- **Welcome (first-stage thinking).** At the start of the interview, state your objective, set the scene and establish your relationship. 'Why are we talking about this matter? Why *us*?' Do whatever you can to help the interviewee relax. Make sure the interviewee understands the rules you are establishing, and agrees to them.

- **Acquire (first-stage thinking).** The second step is information gathering. Concentrate on finding out as much as possible about the matter, as the interviewee sees it. Your task is to listen. Ask questions only to keep the interview on course or to encourage the interviewee further down a useful road. Take care not to judge or imply that you are making any decision.

- **Supply (second-stage thinking).** Now, at the third step, the interview has moved on from information gathering to joint problem solving. Review options for action. It's important at this stage of the interview to remind yourselves of the objective that you set at the start.

- **Part (second-stage thinking).** Finally, make a decision. You and the interviewee work out what you have agreed. State explicitly the interview's outcome: the action that will result from it. The essence of the parting stage is that you explicitly agree what is going to happen next. What is going to happen? Who will do it? Is there a deadline? Who is going to check on progress?

What about after the interview? In many cases, you may need time to put your thoughts in order and make decisions. Indeed, it might be entirely inappropriate to decide – or to tell the interviewee what you have decided – at the end of the interview itself. The interviewee, too, may need time to reflect on the interview. Nevertheless, you must tell the interviewee what you expect the next step to be and make sure that they agree to it.

Three other points are worth remembering at the end of an interview:

■ Make your notes immediately. There's no general rule about whether to take notes *during* the interview, except that note-taking should not interfere with listening to the interviewee unduly.

■ Make sure that you carry out any actions you have agreed at the end of the interview and follow up on actions agreed by the interviewee.

■ Think about your own performance as an interviewer. What went well? What could have been better? Above all, did you achieve the objective you set yourself? A few moments reviewing your own performance can certainly help you in later interviews.

types of interview

These are a selection of the most common interviews you will hold as a manager. Every interview is analysed in terms of the four-stage WASP structure. Whatever kind of interview you are holding, use all the skills of enquiry that we have explored in Chapter 4, namely:

■ paying attention;

■ treating the interviewee as an equal;
■ cultivating ease;
■ encouraging;
■ asking quality questions;
■ rationing information;
■ giving positive feedback.

appraisal

An appraisal interview is one of the most important you hold as a manager. It's vital that both you and the jobholder prepare thoroughly for the interview.

preparing for the interview
You should study the jobholder's job description and the standards of performance that you have set up. If targets have been set and regularly reviewed, think about these with care. The key questions to ask at this stage are as follows:

■ What results has the jobholder achieved?
■ Where has the jobholder exceeded expectations or shown real progress?
■ Which results have not been achieved? Can you suggest why?

Make sure that you tell the jobholder what you are doing to prepare and invite them to prepare in a similar way. Ask them, well in advance, to consider their own performance over the appraised period, and to note successes, failures and anything in between!

The essence of a successful appraisal is the comparison of the two sets of ideas: yours and the jobholder's. You are aiming for shared understanding: an agreement about the jobholder's performance and potential for the future.

holding the interview

Don't kill the appraisal off at an early stage by descending into adversarial conversation. Be ready with the Ladder of Inference (see Chapter 3) to take any potential controversy into a more careful examination of facts and feelings.

welcome

Review standards, targets, the job description and any other aspects of performance that you have both looked at. Relate them: take comparisons and talk about what's been achieved, and what has not happened. Stick to the known facts and make sure that you agree them.

Your questions to the jobholder might include the following:

- How do you feel your job has been going since we last spoke?
- What do you feel you do best?
- Where do you have real problems?
- How relevant is the job description?

acquire

Open up the interview by asking the jobholder for their views and withholding your own. Review the possible reasons for achievement or lack of it. Open up the interview to include matters of competency, skills, training and external circumstances.

Questions at this stage might include the following:

- What are your strong points?
- Where do you think you could develop?
- What particular problems have you had? How do you think you could have handled them differently?

Look for possibilities rather than uttering closed judgements. Instead of saying, for example, 'You're aggressive with our customers', you might say 'Some of our customers seem to perceive your behaviour as aggressive. What do you think about that?'. Use behaviour as the basis for your comments. Have evidence to hand. Be ready to reinterpret the evidence from the jobholder's point of view.

supply

This is the problem-solving part of the interview. Analyse what you have found, and focus on opportunities for action, change and improvement. Generate alternatives. Seek agreement on what could be done. You might be looking for new moves towards targets, performance standards or even amendments to the job description.

Questions at this stage include the following:

- ■ What might we do to alter our targets or standards?
- ■ Do we need to rewrite any part of the job description?
- ■ How could the job be improved? Have you any ideas?

part

You and the jobholder confirm your agreement and part on the clear understanding that these actions are recorded and will be monitored.

Look back at the essential elements of a conversation for action in Chapter 3. Remember that you will gain more commitment from the jobholder if you make requests and invite them to give a considered response.

Don't complete any forms during the interview. It will take too long and distract you from your real business. Take time to fill out any paperwork carefully, after the interview has ended. You need time to assemble your thoughts and summarise them in your mind. You should, of course, at least show any completed paperwork to the jobholder and involve them in any changes.

You must make sure that you carry out any actions that you agree to in the interview: support, procedural changes, delegation or training. If you do not, you undermine both your own authority and the credibility of the appraisal process itself. And you will find it harder next time to generate the respect and trust that form the basis of the whole system.

handling poor performance

You will sometimes have to handle poor performance. Anyone can perform under par at times. Usually some underachieving can be tolerated, but persistent or serious shortfalls need action. Avoiding the issue will not make it go away.

What you may see as poor performance is not necessarily the jobholder's fault. In fact, it's unrewarding to think in terms of blame or fault if you detect poor performance. Of course, it may be a genuine case of misconduct; but the circumstances of poor performance are likely to be more complex. An effective manager will look deeper and not jump to conclusions.

First, establish the gap. What is the standard that isn't being met? Is the gap sufficient enough, and consistent enough, to warrant action?

Now establish possible reasons for the gap in achievement. There are three main reasons why jobholders can under perform:

■ **Domestic circumstances.** They may be in poor health or suffering some emotional instability, owing to family or personal problems.

■ **Poor management.** The job has not been sufficiently explained. Planning has been poor. The job may have changed in ways that don't make sense to the jobholder. Resources may be lacking. Discipline may be slack. Physical conditions may make working to standard very difficult. You may be managing the job poorly – as may another manager.

■ **Lack of organisational 'fit'.** The jobholder may be unhappy in the team, or the team unhappy with the jobholder. So-called 'personality clashes' may be getting in the way, or a sense of natural justice may be being abused.

Having established the gap and the reason for it, you must set out with the jobholder to work out a plan for closing the gap. Where are the opportunities for improvement? How might you be able to help? Think of this part of the interview as joint problem solving. Find a course of action that the jobholder can agree to. Only they can behave differently, so they must decide what to do. They may be able to make substantial improvements in stages. Explain that you will be available to help.

Record your agreement and don't forget to follow up on agreed action.

delegation

Delegation is deliberately choosing to give somebody authority to do something you could do yourself. It is not just 'handing out work'. You give somebody a responsibility: the task to be performed; and you devolve authority: the power to make other decisions and to take action to carry out the responsibility. Successful delegation involves matching responsibility with authority. Anybody who manages will know how difficult this can be – as will any parent or carer.

preparing for the interview: working out what to delegate

Review your own objectives. Now distinguish between the activities you can delegate and those for which you must take personal responsibility. Obvious candidates for delegation include:

- routine tasks;
- time-consuming tasks – research, testing, administrative or co-ordinating activities;
- complete tasks that can be delegated as a block of work;
- communication tasks – letters, promotional material, telephone calls.

Delegate tasks that might be tedious for you but prove a real challenge to somebody else. Do not delegate:

- tasks completely beyond the skills and experience of the person concerned;
- strategic, policy, confidential or security matters;
- tasks involving discipline over the person's peers.

Having decided what to delegate, ask these questions:

- What skills, experience, expertise and qualifications are necessary for the task?
- Whose skills profile best matches the need?
- What further training or support would be necessary?

Look for people's interest in work that they haven't already done, or have maybe shown some aptitude for in unusual circumstances (covering for somebody else, coping in a crisis). Look for abilities that are exercised elsewhere: in another part of their work, or perhaps outside work.

holding the interview

As with other kinds of interview, you can structure the interview to give yourself the best possible chance of success.

- **Welcome.** Explain the purpose of the interview. Begin by making the request. 'I should like to discuss with you the possibility of delegating x.' Explain the task you are considering delegating, and why you have thought of the interviewee as the best person to do the task. Explain that their position is an open one: they should feel under no obligation until they have clearly understood the question you are asking.
- **Acquire.** Ask the jobholder to explore their understanding of the issue and how they might see themselves relating to it. Does it fit with other

responsibilities that they currently carry? Can they see it as an opportunity to grow and develop new skills? Examine, too, the standards of performance. Are they appropriate or attainable? Would training be necessary?

■ **Supply.** Explore with the jobholder the opportunities for taking on this new task. This is joint problem-solving again, looking at the new arrangement in terms of how it might work, how you might help and how the interviewee might make the work more their own.

■ **Part.** Now make your request a formal one. Give timescales or deadlines, as well as conditions of satisfaction: standards or targets to be achieved, how you will monitor progress and check for success.

Make it clear to the delegate that they have four possible responses:

■ They can accept the request and make a commitment: 'I promise that I will do x by time y.'
■ They can decline. They must be free to say 'No', while at the same time being clear of the consequences of a refusal.
■ They can decide to commit later. 'I'll get back to you by time z, when I will give you a definite response.'
■ They can make a counter offer. 'I'm not willing to do x; however, I can promise you that I will do w (or maybe part of x) by time y.'

The result of this interview should be a clear commitment by the delegate to action: to the task originally intended for delegation, to part of the task, to another task, or to refusal.

In accepting a newly delegated responsibility, the delegate must be clear about three limits on their action:

- **Objectives.** The broad objectives of the task, the specific targets, conditions of satisfaction and timescales should all be made explicit.
- **Policy.** 'Rules and regulations.' The manner in which the task is carried out must conform to any legal, contractual or policy guidelines under which the organisation operates.
- **Limits of authority.** This is critically important. The delegate must know clearly where their authority extends and where it ends: what powers they have for hiring or using staff, their budgetary authority, the resources available to them, their access to information, their power to take decisions without referral.

Finally, you as the manager must give the delegate full confidence to do the task. Make it plain that you will:

- give any support that you or they consider necessary;
- provide any training that may be needed;
- be available for consultation or advice;
- make the delegation public knowledge.

coaching

Coaching is improving performance. The aim of a coaching interview is to help the coachee think for themselves, fostering greater awareness and hence greater responsibility. Fostering awareness is the first stage of coaching and involves looking at:

- what is going on;
- the goals;
- dynamics and relationships between the coachee and others;
- wider organisational issues;
- the coachee's own feelings; fears, emotions, desires, intuitions, capabilities.

Fostering responsibility is the second stage of coaching and involves second-stage thinking: thinking about what to do. So at this stage, coaching encourages the coachee to think about:

- ideas for action;
- opportunities for change or growth;
- deciding what to do and how to do it;
- taking action.

The essence of the coach's role is to ask questions. Instructing will tend to generate a minimal response: the action carried out, but little more. Asking a question focuses attention, increases awareness and encourages the coachee to take responsibility. Asking questions also helps the coach. Instead of forging ahead with a sequence of orders, the coach can use questions to follow the coachee's train of thought, their interest or enthusiasm, their emotional reactions – and adapt the coaching accordingly.

The most effective questions are those that encourage the coachee to think for themselves. Questions that point up the coachee's ignorance or subservience are unhelpful. The best coaching questions are open, non-judgemental and *specific*. Use the 'W' questions: 'What? Where? When? Who? How many? How much?'. Avoid 'Why?' and 'How?'. They will tend to imply judgement, analysis or criticism: all of them forms of second-stage thinking. If necessary, 'Why?' can become 'What were the reasons for' and 'How?' might be better put as 'What were the steps that...?'.

During second-stage thinking, the same kinds of questions can serve to focus on what the coachee will do next, how, when, where and so on.

The Ladder of Inference is a useful tool in this process. Walking the coachee down the ladder from beliefs or assumptions to specific observations will encourage a wider awareness; walking up the ladder through meanings, judgement and belief to action will strengthen motivation and a sense of responsibility for future actions.

holding the interview

There are four parts to the coaching process. The WASP interview structure now takes on a new name, based around the word GROW:

- ■ **Goal** setting: for the session and for the coachee's development;
- ■ **Reality** analysis, to explore the current situation for difficulties and opportunities;
- ■ **Options** for future courses of action;
- ■ **What** to do: a 'hard' decision on action, **When** and by **Whom**.

goal setting

The initial task is to decide the purpose of the coaching: to establish your goal, both for the coaching session itself and for the performance issue being coached.

Think of the coachee's goals as statements beginning 'How to...'. Generate as many new 'How to' statements as you can from the original goal. This helps you to explore the coachee's deeper values, their higher aspirations and longer-term ambitions.

Now categorise these numerous 'How to' statements. Some will be 'end goals'; others will be 'performance goals', measurable levels of performance that may set you on the path to an end goal or prove that you've achieved it. All of them are revealing: but you will only be able to choose one or two for immediate coaching. The best goals to choose, for practical purposes, are those that generate the greatest creative tension between goal and reality. Like the tension in a taut elastic band that stores potential energy, it is creative tension that will provide the energy for movement. Which goals excite the coachee most? Which generate the most commitment?

reality checking

Creative tension depends as much on a clear perception of

reality as on a clear goal. Look reality coolly in the face. Be objective; avoid judgement. Instead of describing past performance, for example, as 'bad' or 'inadequate', focus on the specific aspects of it that need improvement. Walk the coachee down the Ladder of Inference and offer verifiable, measurable observations:

- ■ 'What have you tried so far?'
- ■ 'What were the results?'
- ■ 'Exactly how much under target did you come in?'
- ■ 'What resources do you lack?'
- ■ 'When did you last check the situation?'
- ■ 'Where were the actual difficulties?'

Remember that a good deal of current reality is inner reality. Follow where the coachee's concerns take you and (gently) investigate their emotional responses.

- ■ 'How did you feel when you tried...?'
- ■ 'What emotions arise when you talk about...?'
- ■ 'Is there anything you're afraid of?'
- ■ 'How do you think you might be preventing yourself from achieving more?'

options for action

This is potentially the most creative part of the coaching process. Your purpose here is to find as many options for action as possible, in order to choose specific, realistic 'next steps'.

'The opponent within one's own head' can be a powerful censor:

- ■ 'It can't be done.'
- ■ 'We can't do it like that.'
- ■ 'They would never agree to it.'
- ■ 'It will be too expensive.'

■ 'Altogether too risky/disruptive/complicated/radical.'
■ 'I don't have the time.'
■ 'That's already been tried – and look what happened.'

You might counter these objections with 'What if' questions:

■ 'What if we could do it?'
■ 'What if this barrier didn't exist?'
■ 'What if we could get them to agree?'
■ 'What if we found a budget?'
■ 'What if we managed the risk/minimised disruption/ made it simpler...?'
■ 'What if we reallocated resources?'
■ 'What if we tried again?'

Keep your options open:

■ 'What else could you do?'
■ 'Could you do it differently?'
■ 'Are there other ways of meeting this target or goal?'

Carefully examine the costs and benefits of the action; list its positive, negative and interesting aspects. Don't limit yourselves to one option: perhaps you can merge two or more as a realistic course of action, or schedule options as immediate and longer term.

what to do

This part of the coaching process is about drawing up a detailed action plan:

■ 'What are you going to do?'
■ 'When will you do it?'
■ 'Will this action (or series of actions) move you towards your goal?'

■ 'What barriers might you have to overcome?'
■ 'Who else will be involved?'
■ 'What support do you need? Where will you find it?'
■ 'What other consequences are there of this course of action, and how do we deal with them?'

And it is vital for the coach to ask a final question:

■ 'What can I do to help?'

It is a good idea to document the agreed action plan, and even sign it, to confirm that the coachee is committed to carrying it through. Build in a review date to monitor progress.

counselling

Counselling, like coaching, helps someone to help themselves. Unlike coaching, you are not helping to develop a skill, but rather helping to resolve a situation that the person sees as a problem.

Counselling is not giving advice. As a counsellor, your role is to provide a different perspective from which to try out ideas. The counselled person (I suppose we must call them the 'counsellee'!) must find their own solution and exercise their own responsibility. Neither the counsellor nor the counsellee knows the answer at the start of the counselling interview. The answer emerges from the interview itself.

Counselling always relies on the assumption that the counsellee has the skills, knowledge and – deep down – the desire to find a solution. It also assumes that these skills and qualities are impeded in some way. The impediment may be no more than the belief that the counsellee doesn't know what to do.

the skills of counselling
The skills of counselling are not unlike the skills you use every day when people tell you about their problems. The difference

is that you must behave professionally; in other words, honestly, consistently, and without prejudice. Your contribution should be well informed and appropriate to the situation.

Counselling, more than any other managerial interview, demands deep listening skills. Indeed, you may be required to do nothing but listen. Beyond the essential skill of listening, there are two main skills that come to the fore in counselling:

■ reflecting;
■ confronting.

Used well, they will all help to make the interview more productive.

reflecting

Counsellors use reflection in three main ways. They reflect:

■ what people seem to be feeling;
■ their words, the content of what they have said;
■ the implied content.

They are such a vital tool of counselling that it is worth looking at each of them separately.

reflecting feelings This is probably the most useful, and the technique likely to be used first in a counselling session. It always clarifies the issue being discussed and it helps the speaker to know that the listener really does understand. Frequently it needs to be no more than a few words:

■ 'You feel angry.'
■ 'You seem to be distracted.'
■ 'Perhaps you are confused.'

reflecting the speaker's words This is a very simple and effective technique, enabling you to prompt the counsellee

without running the risk of the discussion 'going off track'.
Early in a session, it can 'open up issues', at other times it can
help to break through a 'block'. The counsellor listens carefully
for emotionally charged words, those given undue emphasis, or
for which the speaker's voice fades or becomes barely audible.
Simply repeating those words can have magical effects.

reflecting content   The trick here is simply to repeat what the
counsellee has just told you: 'You say that you are not being
challenged enough.' It usually results in an elaboration of the
point that has been made and provides a way forward. Perhaps
the counsellee can't quite bring themselves to say it, but they
will talk volubly on the subject if you legitimise it for them.

confronting

Use this technique with great care. It may consist simply of
asking for concrete detail to support an allegation or an expression
of vague feeling. It may involve pointing out apparent
contradictions: between what the counsellee is saying and what
they said earlier; between what they are saying and the way
they are saying it; between words and body language.
Remember that you are confronting perceptions in order to
root out possible new ones. You are not confronting to criticise
or to degrade the counsellee in any way.

holding the interview

The four stages of counselling are very like those of coaching.
The main difference between them is a matter of emphasis.
Coaching is about reaching a goal and improving in some way;
counselling is essentially about removing some obstacle or
difficulty and simply being able to move on.

welcome

You need to establish at the outset a positive relationship
between counsellor and counsellee. The counsellee will almost

certainly be feeling vulnerable and anything you can do to put them at their ease – to create the trust and respect that they need – is essential. Ask 'What is the problem?' (as the counsellee sees it), 'Where is the "blockage"?'.

acquire

Some aspect of this problem is probably 'buried': either because the counsellee is unwilling to bring it to the surface (for fear of the consequences) or because they are not aware of it. Help them to step back and examine the possibilities of the situation by asking questions such as:

'Why do you think you feel this way?'
'What kind of response do you think you might get if you told X about this?'
'Who else has contributed to the problem?'
'How do you think this has arisen?'
'What might be the cause of the problem?'

You might consider making the interview more creative at this stage by asking the counsellee to think about the problem in radically different ways.

'What does this problem look like?'
'If you were the problem, how would you feel?'
'Can you think of another way of expressing the problem?'

In some situations, you may be able to help the counsellee to transform the problem in some radical way. They probably see the problem as a burden that they must bear or an obstacle that they must overcome. A key stage in taking ownership of the problem is to see it instead as a goal for which they can take responsibility.

Invite the counsellee to try to frame the problem as a 'How to' statement. The idea is that by doing so the problem becomes expressed as an objective: a way forward that the counsellee might want to take. A 'How to' statement also implies multiple possibilities of movement: if you are asking 'how to' achieve a goal, the mind immediately responds with 'well, you might... or you might...' and so on.

Turning an obstacle into a goal is at the very heart of the counselling process. You must use all your skill and sensitivity to manage this most crucial part of the process. A counsellee may all too easily feel pressure at this point to take ownership of a problem when they have no desire to.

supply

Now you must supply some possible courses of action and consider their consequences. The counsellee should be moving from emotion to a more considered attitude without any pressure from you. They should be visualising various results and how they would feel about them. They should be feeling more enabled to choose a course of action.

part

At this last stage of the counselling interview, you are not making a request – beyond the simple request that the counsellee makes a decision. Now that they can see their situation more clearly and have assessed various options, they need to make a move. It might be a very small one; it might be the beginnings of a planned strategy. (Many of my own more stressful problems seem to dissolve in the face of a clear plan.)

If you have helped someone to make a clear plan that they are motivated to act on, then your counselling has succeeded. You can also use this stage of the interview to help the counsellee reflect on the skills, knowledge, experience and personal qualities that are likely to help them through.

making a presentation

Think of a presentation as a formal conversation. Speaking to groups is a notoriously stressful activity. Most people spend hours of their time holding conversations. Something strange seems to happen, however, when they're called upon to talk to a group of people formally. A host of irrational – and maybe not so irrational fears – raise their ugly heads. Ask anyone to make a presentation and many people would do all they can to wriggle out of it.

what do you fear most?

A recent study in the United States asked people about their deepest fears. The results were interesting. Here they are, in order:

- speaking to groups;
- heights;
- insects and bugs;
- financial problems;
- deep water;
- sickness;

■ death;
■ flying;
■ loneliness;
■ dogs.
(From *The Book of Lists*, David Wallechinsky)

I think that one of the main causes of this anxiety is that you put yourself on the spot when you present. The audience will be judging, not just your ideas and your evidence, but you as well. People may not remember reports or spreadsheets easily, but a presentation can make a powerful impression that lasts. If the presenter seemed nervous, incompetent or ill-informed, that reputation will stick – at least until the next presentation.

You, the presenter, are at the heart of it. An effective presenter puts themself centre-stage. An ineffective presenter tries to hide behind notes, a lectern, slides or computer-generated graphics. To become more effective, you need to take control of the three core elements of the event, namely:

■ the material;
■ the audience;
■ yourself.

Whatever you are presenting, you will also need to use all the skills of persuasion that we explored in Chapter 5:

■ working out your big idea: your message;
■ validating your message using SPQR (see Chapter 5);
■ arranging your ideas coherently;
■ expressing your ideas vividly;
■ remembering your ideas;
■ delivering well.

putting yourself on show

Think a bit more about this business of nerves. What's going on in those minutes and hours before you stand up and make your presentation? What is your body saying?

That nervous, jittery feeling is caused by adrenalin. This is a hormone secreted by your adrenal glands (near your kidneys). Adrenalin causes your arteries to constrict, which increases your blood pressure and stimulates the heart. Why stimulate the heart? To give you extra energy. When do you need extra energy? When you're in danger. Adrenalin release is an evolved response to threat. When that sabre-toothed tiger had you cornered, you needed as much energy as possible, either to hurl the spear or to run. Now that sabre-tooths are no more, this useful hormonal response is still available to give you energy at times of crisis.

Adrenalin has two other effects. It increases your concentration – particularly useful when making a presentation. Less usefully, adrenalin also stimulates excretion of body waste. This decreases your body weight, giving you a slight advantage when it comes to running! That's why you want to visit the toilet immediately before presenting.

Your anxiety is probably more about your relationship with the audience than about what you have to say. In the moments before you present, you may find yourself suffering from one or more of the following conditions:

■ demophobia – a fear of people;
■ laliophobia – a fear of speaking;
■ katagelophobia – a fear of ridicule.

Check your condition against this list of adrenalin-related symptoms:

■ rapid pulse;

- ■ shallow breathing;
- ■ muscle spasms in the throat, knees and hands;
- ■ dry mouth;
- ■ cold extremities;
- ■ dilated pupils;
- ■ sweaty palms;
- ■ blurred vision;
- ■ nausea.

And the worst of it is that, however much you suffer, the audience will forget virtually everything you say! That's the bad news. The good news is that you're not alone. Every presenter – indeed, every performer – suffers from nerves. Many actors and musicians talk about the horror of nerves and the fact that experience never seems to make them better.

The best news is that nerves are there to help you. They are telling you that this presentation matters – and that *you* matter. You are the medium through which the audience will understand your ideas. You *should* feel nervous. If you don't, you aren't taking the presentation seriously and you are in danger of letting your concentration slip.

preparing for the presentation

The trick is not to try to dispel the nerves, but to use them. Once you understand that nervousness is natural, and indeed necessary, it becomes a little easier to handle.

Everyone is frightened of the unknown. Any presentation involves an element of uncertainty, because it's 'live'. You can't plan for the audience's mood on the day. You may not even be able to foresee who will be there. You can't plan for any sudden development that affects the proposal or explanation you are giving. You can't plan for every question that you might be asked. This is, of course, the greatest strength of presentations: you and the audience are together, in the same place, at the same time. You are bringing the material alive for them, here and now. If nothing is left to chance, the presentation will remain dead on the floor.

The trick is to know what to leave to chance. If you can support your nerves with solid preparation, you can channel your nervous energy into the performance itself. Prepare well, and you will be ready to bring the presentation to life.

You can prepare in three areas:

1. the material;
2. the audience;
3. yourself.

In each case, preparation means taking control. If you can remove the element of uncertainty in these areas, you will be ready to encounter what can't be controlled: the instantaneous and living relationship between you and your audience.

managing the material

Taking control of the material is best done systematically. Many presentations fail not because the presenter is weak, but because the material is disorderly. The audience tries its utmost to understand, but gets lost. You have to remember that they will forget virtually everything you say. They may remember rather more of what you show them, but only if it is quite simple. Don't expect any audience to remember, from the presentation alone, more than half a dozen ideas.

In presentations, more than in any other kind of corporate communication, you must *display the shape of your thinking*. That shape will only be clear if you keep it simple. Detail doesn't make things clearer; it makes things more complicated. If you want to display the shape of your thinking, you must design it. Managing the material is a design process.

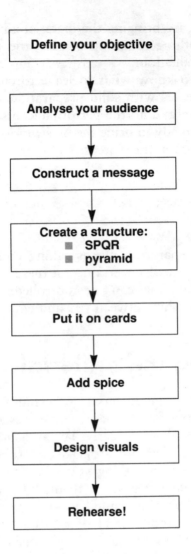

Figure 7.1

defining your objective

Why are you making this presentation? That's the first, and most important, question you must answer. Everything else –

the material you include, its order, the level of detail you go into, how long the presentation will last, what visual aids you will use – will depend on your answer to this question.

What do you want your audience to take away at the end of the presentation? More importantly: what do you want them to do? Your objective is to tell them everything they need to know to take that action – and nothing more.

Why is it a presentation? You could write a report, send a batch of e-mails, write a memo, put up posters, put an article in your organisation's newsletter, print a thousand leaflets, make a video, hold a series of meetings or even make a CD ROM. Why are you going to the trouble of gathering a group of people together in one place, booking the room, setting up the equipment and putting yourself through the torture of making a presentation?

I believe that there's only one reason why you should be making a presentation. It may sound rather grand, but presentations are meant to inspire your audience. Your task is to bring your ideas alive with your own feelings, your own commitment, your own passion. It's that belief that the audience is looking for. And if you act as if you don't believe in what you are saying, the audience won't believe it either.

So, your objective must be to inspire your audience. If you have any other objective, choose another method of communication. If you are simply making a pronouncement and not seeking or expecting any kind of response, you may as well write it down. For teaching or instructing, you will need to adapt a presentation into a much more interactive activity. Above all, if you want to deliver detailed information, a presentation is about the worst communication method you could choose. Your audience will simply forget all the detail. Yet many presenters continue to make the fundamental mistake of packing presentations with masses of detailed facts and figures, often on overhead or computer-generated slides, unsupported by any printouts.

Write your objective down in one sentence. This helps you to:

■ clear your mind;
■ select material to fit;
■ check at the end of planning that you are still addressing a single clear issue.

Write a simple sentence beginning:

'The aim of this presentation is to...'

Make sure the verb following that word 'to' is suitably inspirational!

analysing your audience

Your presentation will be successful if the audience feels that you have spoken directly to them. If you can demonstrate that you have tailored your material to their needs, the audience will be more inclined to accept it.

So think about your audience carefully:

■ How many will there be?
■ What is their status range?
■ Will they want to be there?
■ How much do they already know about the matter? How much more do they need to know?
■ What will they be expecting? What is the history, the context, the rumour, the gossip?
■ How does your message and your material relate to the audience? Relevance defines what you will research, include and highlight. It will also help you to decide where to start: what your point of entry will be.
■ Is the audience young or old? Are they predominantly one gender or mixed?

■ Are they technical specialists or generalists? They will want different levels of detail.

■ Where are they in the organisation? Different working groups will have different interests and different ways of looking at the world.

Think, too, about the audience's expectations of the presentation. They may see presentations often, or very rarely. They may also have specific expectations of you, the presenter: they may know you well or hardly at all; you may have some sort of reputation that goes before you.

---

match or exceed your audience's expectations

Broadly, your audience has certain expectations, of you and of itself. How will you meet these, or exceed them? You may, of course, want to confound their expectations: but this may be a little risky!

Audience's expectations of you	Audience's expectations of itself
Set direction and pace	To be led
Be competent	To work at the speaker's pace
Know your stuff	To be told what to do (take notes, ask questions, etc)
Be confident	

---

constructing a message

Once you have your objective, and you have some sense of who your audience is, you can begin to plan your material. Begin with a clear message. This should have all the characteristics of the messages that we looked at in Chapter 5. Your message must:

■ be a sentence;
■ express your objective;
■ contain a single idea;
■ have no more than 15 words;
■ grab your audience's attention.

You might consider putting this message on to a slide or other visual aid and show it near the start of the presentation. But an effective message should be able to stick in the mind without any help. Make your message as vivid as you can.

creating a structure

Everything in the structure of the presentation should support your message. Remember to keep the structure of your presentation *simple*. The audience will forget most of what you say to them. Make sure that they remember your message and a few key points.

weaving an introduction

Use SPQR (see Chapter 5) to start the presentation, leading the audience from where they are to where you want them to be. This also allows you to show that you understand their situation and that you are there to help them. Using SPQR will convince them that you have put yourself into their shoes. The more obvious the problem is to the audience, the less time you will need to spend on SPQR.

SPQR also allows you to demonstrate your own credentials for being there. Your values and beliefs are what make you credible to the audience: remember, they are judging you as well as what you have to say. What qualifies you to speak on this subject? What special experience or expertise do you have? How can you add value to the ideas in your presentation? Your own values and beliefs will be more credible if you can weave them into a story. SPQR gives you the structure. You could begin your presentation by telling a brief story, making sure that your audience will be able to relate to it. Stories have a way of sticking in the mind long after arguments have faded. Choose a story that demonstrates your values in relation to the matter in hand. Beware generalised sentiment. Avoid 'motherhood and apple pie' stories. Make the story authentic and relevant. And keep it brief. You need to allow as much time as possible for your new ideas.

building a pyramid

Use a pyramid structure to outline your small number of key points. Show the pyramid visually: an overhead or PowerPoint slides, or a flip chart. Indicate that these key points will form the sections of the presentation.

Repetition is an essential feature of good presentations. Because the audience can't re-read or rewind to remind themselves of what you said, you need to build their recall by repeating the key features of your presentation. The key features will be your message, your structure, your key points and any call to action that you deliver at the end. Aim to build the audience's recall on no more than about half-a-dozen pieces of information.

Most people seem to know the famous *tell 'em* principle:

■ Tell 'em what you're going to tell 'em.
■ Tell 'em.
■ Tell 'em what you've told 'em.

This valuable technique is one you should use often in your presentation. Build the three-part repetition into the presentation as a whole: tell 'em at the start what the whole presentation will cover; and tell 'em at the end what the whole thing has covered. Use the technique, too, within each part of the presentation: summarising at the start and end, so that you lead the audience into and out of each section explicitly.

Don't be afraid to repeat your ideas. If you want the audience to remember them, you can't repeat them too often.

If you plan well, you will almost certainly create too much

material. You must now decide what to leave out, and what you could leave out if necessary. Be ruthless. Bear in mind that your audience will forget most of what you say. Go back to your pyramid and make sure that you have enough time to cover each key point. Weed out any detail that will slow you down or divert you from your objective.

opening and closing the presentation

Once the body of the presentation is in place, you need to design an opening and close that will help you take off and land safely. You need to be able to perform these on 'autopilot'. Memorise them word for word or write them out in full.

The opening of your presentation should include:

- introducing yourself – who you are and why you are there;
- acknowledging the audience – thanking them for their time and recognising what they are expecting;
- a clear statement of your objective or, better still, your message;
- a timetable – finish times, breaks if necessary;
- rules and regulations – note-taking, how you will take questions;
- any 'housekeeping' items – safety, refreshments, administration.

Once these elements are in place, you can decide exactly how to order the items. You might decide to start with something surprising or unusual: launching into a story or a striking example, seemingly improvising some remark about the venue or immediate circumstances of your talk, asking a question. Sometimes it's a good idea to talk with the audience at the very start before launching into the presentation proper.

The close of the presentation is the most memorable moment. Whatever else happens, the audience will almost certainly remember this! This is your last chance to 'tell 'em what you've told 'em'. Summarise your key points, and your message. Just as composers often aim to finish a piece of music on a loud note, you can aim to end your presentation 'on a bang not a whimper'. Give a call to action. Talk about the advantages or benefits to the audience of your ideas, and show how they can – or should – put them into action. Be specific in your call to action: what exactly do you want the audience to do?

Thank the audience for their attention. You might also formally guide them into a question session, giving them time to relax after concentrating and perhaps pre-arranging a 'planted question' in the audience to set the ball rolling.

putting it on cards

Put your ideas on to cards. These are useful memory devices and will help you to bring the presentation alive.

The best presentations are given without notes. But few people will always have the confidence or experience to be able to deliver without any help. Nevertheless, any notes you create should aim to support your memory, not substitute for it.

Don't write your presentation out in full unless you are an accomplished actor. Only actors can make recitation sound convincing – and nobody is asking you to act. Use cards. Filing or archive cards are best; use the largest you can find. Cards have a number of key advantages:

- They are less shaky than paper – they don't rustle.
- They are more compact.
- They give your hands something firm to hold.
- They can be tagged with a treasury tag to prevent loss of order.
- They look more professional.
- They force you to write only brief notes.

By writing only brief notes, triggers and cues on your cards, you force yourself to think about what you are saying, while you are saying it. This means that you will sound much more convincing. Obviously, your audience will only tolerate a certain amount of silence while you think of the next thing to say. The note on the card is there to trigger that next point and keep you moving.

Write your notes in bold print, using pen or felt-tip. Write on only one side and number the cards sequentially. Include:

- what you *must* say;
- what you *should* say to support the main idea;
- what you *could* say if you have time.

Add notes on timing, visual aids, cues for your own behaviour. Keep the cards simple to look at and rehearse with them so that you get to know them.

adding spice

Exciting presentations bring ideas alive. You are the medium through which the audience understands the material. You must make the presentation your own and give it the spicy smell of real life.

Rack your brain for anything you can use. Think it up, cook it up, dream it up if necessary. Look for:

- images;
- examples;
- analogies;
- stories;
- pictures;
- jokes (but be very careful about these).

The aim is to create pictures in your audience's mind. Don't let PowerPoint do it all for you. And don't fall into the trap of thinking that putting text on a visual aid makes it visual. Your audience wants *images*: real pictures, not words.

The most powerful pictures are the ones you can conjure up in your audience's imagination with your own words. There's a famous story about a little girl who claimed she liked plays on the radio, 'because the pictures were better'. You should be aiming to create such pictures in your audience's mind.

designing visuals

Working on the visuals can take longer than any other part of the planning. The important thing to remember is that any aid you use is there to help you, not to substitute for you. You are not a voice-over accompanying a slide presentation; the pictures are there to illustrate your ideas. The audience wants to see you: to meet with you, assess you, ask you questions, learn about you. They will not have the chance to do any of this if you hide behind your visual aids.

Many audiences now seem to expect flashy, computer-generated slides. Presenters feel obliged to spend days putting together a sequence filled with animation effects. So, confound their expectations. Use the technology by all means – and then leap away from it, galvanising your audience with your own passion for your subject.

Visual aids intrude. The moment you turn on the projector or turn to the flip chart, the audience's attention is on that rather than you. A small number of excellent visual aids will have far more impact than a large number of indifferent ones. Don't fall into the trap of thinking that every part of the presentation should have an accompanying slide. You should be able to do without these things for 80 per cent of the time.

Avoid information overload. This means:

■ use just a few visuals;
■ display only *one idea* on each.

Remove any detail from a picture or chart that you don't need the audience to read. The guiding principle is: make the graphic at least twice as simple and four times as bold as anything you would put in a report. Don't simply transfer a spreadsheet or table on to a slide. Simplify.

Try to avoid putting words on to any visual aid. This probably sounds almost absurd. What? No words at all? Well: no, not if you can manage it. Words are for listening to. Visual aids are for looking at. It really is that simple.

If you must put words on to a visual aid, keep the number ruthlessly down. Aim for headlines and no more. Again and again you will see slides that contain too much text, or complex tables of numbers. Some presenters persist in photocopying a page from a book and using that as a slide!

a style guide for visual aids

- Keep the slides looking consistent in font and overall design.
- Use colour rather than black and white. Consider using white on a coloured background.
- Contrasting colours look most effective.
- Add a corporate logo.
- Use icons, drawn figures and 'clip art' with care: they are already looking like clichés.
- Keep scales and numbering systems simple and consistent.
- Round off numbers: make 45.7 per cent into 46 per cent, and so on.
- Select only the data that supports your argument. Remember that you may be accused of being 'economical with the truth' (though of course that's exactly what any presentation should be).

rehearsing

There is a world of difference between thinking your presentation through and doing it. You may think you know what you want to say, but until you say it you don't really know. Only by uttering it aloud can you test whether you understand what you are saying. Rehearsal is the reality check.

Rehearsal is also a time check. Time acts oddly in presentations. It can seem to stop, to drag and – more often than not – to race away. The most common time problem I encounter with trainees who are rehearsing their presentations is that they run out of time. They are astounded when I tell them that time is up and they have hardly finished introducing themselves! You *must* rehearse to see how long it all takes. Be aware that it will probably take longer than you anticipate: maybe 50 per cent longer.

rehearsing: general guidelines

- Rehearse in real time: don't skip bits.
- Rehearse with a friend. Ask them what they think and work with them to improve.
- Rehearse with your notes. Get into the habit of looking up from them.
- Rehearse with the visual aids at least once.
- Rehearse in the venue itself if you can. If you can't, try to spend some time there, getting the feel of the room.

The ultimate aim of rehearsal is to give you freedom in the presentation itself. Once you have run through the presentation a few times, you will be able to concentrate on the most important element of the event; your relationship with the audience. Under-rehearsed presenters spend too much time working out what to say. Well-rehearsed presenters know what to say and can improvise on it according to the demands of the moment.

You can over-rehearse. If rehearsal means that you become an automaton, it is counterproductive. This is most likely to happen after a number of repetitions of the same presentation. Try to think of each presentation as brand new. After all, it's probably new for this particular audience. They haven't heard your stories or arguments before. They are going on this journey for the first time. Change the material a little each time you present. Think of a new story or a new example.

You must also rehearse with any equipment that you intend to use. Nothing is more nerve-wracking than trying to present with a projector or laptop you've never seen before. Rehearse also to improve your use of the equipment:

■ Talk without support. Don't use the visuals as a crib.
■ Don't talk to visuals. They can't hear you. Avoid turning your back on the audience.
■ Don't let the light of the visuals put you in darkness.
■ Make sure you know how to put things right if they go wrong.
■ If you can, be ready to present without any visual aids at all.

controlling the audience

Many presenters concentrate so hard on the material that they ignore the audience. They have no idea of the messages that their body is sending out. They are thinking so hard about *what* they are saying that they have no time to think about *how* they say it.

You are performing. Your whole body is involved. You must become aware of what your body is doing so that you can control it, and thus the audience. A few basic principles will ensure that you keep the audience within your control.

eye contact

You speak more with your eyes than with your voice. Your eyes tell the audience that you are taking notice of them, that you are confident to speak to them, that you know what you are talking about and that you believe what you are saying.

Look at the audience's eyes throughout the presentation. Imagine that a lighthouse beam is shooting out from your eyes and roving the audience. Make sure that the beam enters every pair of eyes in the room. Focus for a few seconds on each pair of eyes and meet their gaze. Don't look past them, through them or over their heads. Pick out a few faces that look particularly friendly and return to them. After a while, you may even feel confident enough to return to a few of the less friendly ones!

Include the whole audience with your eyes. Many presenters fall into the trap of focusing on only one person: the most senior manager, the strongest personality, maybe simply someone they like a lot.

Keep your cue cards in your hand so that you can easily glance down at them and bring your eyes back to the audience quickly.

your face

The rest of your face is important, too! Remember to smile. Animate your face and remember to make everything just a little larger than life so that your face can be 'read' at the back of the room.

gestures

Many presenters worry about how much or little they gesture. This is reasonable. Arms and hands are prominent parts of the body and can sometimes get out of control.

The important thing is to find the gestures that are natural for you. If you are a great gesticulator, don't try to force your hands into rigid stillness. If you don't normally gesture a great deal, don't force yourself into balletic movements. Use your hands to paint pictures and to help you get the words out. Keep your gestures open, away from your body and into the room. Don't cross your hands behind your back or in front of your crotch, and don't put them in your pockets too much. (It's a good idea to empty your pockets before the presentation so that you don't find yourself jingling coins or keys.)

movement

Aim for stillness. This doesn't mean that you should stand completely still all the time. Moving about the room shows that you are making the space your own, and helps to energise the space between you and the audience. But rhythmic, repetitive movement can be annoying and suggest the neurotic pacing of a panther in a cage. Try not to rock on your feet or tie your legs in knots! Aim to have both feet on the ground as much as possible and slow down your movements.

It can sometimes help to sit to present. You might practise with a chair, or the back of a chair, a stool or even the edge of a table. Make sure that it is stable and solid enough to bear your weight!

looking after yourself

And you will *still* be nervous as the moment of truth approaches. Remember that those nerves are there to help you. If you have prepared adequately, you should be ready to use them to encounter the uncertainty of live performance.

You certainly need time before presenting that is quiet and focused. I need to spend about 15 minutes doing nothing but preparing myself mentally. I put myself where nothing can distract me from the presentation. Visualising success immediately before the presentation works for some people. Ahead of time, imagine yourself presenting, the audience attentively listening to your every word, applauding you at the end and asking keen questions afterwards.

On some occasions it can be useful to meet the audience and chat with them before you start. This can break the ice and put you more at ease. In truth, I only rarely feel comfortable doing this; for others, it can be highly beneficial in relaxing them and preparing for the presentation.

The most important preparation involves breathing. Make contact with the deepest kind of breathing, that works from the stomach rather than the upper part of the lungs. Slow that breathing down, and make it calm, regular and strong. This works wonders for the voice: it gives it depth and power, and makes for a more convincing delivery.

Along with your breathing, pay attention to the muscles around your mouth that help you to articulate. Try some tongue-twisters or sing a favourite song. Chew the cud, and get your tongue and lips really working and warmed up. A very simple exercise is to stick your tongue as far out of your mouth as you can and then speak a part of your presentation, trying to make the consonants as clear as you can. You only need to do this for about 30 seconds to wake up your voice and make it clearer. You will, of course, look rather silly while doing this, so it's best to do the exercise in a private place!

answering questions

Many presenters are as worried about the question session as about the presentation itself. A few guidelines can help to turn your question session from a trial into a triumph:

- ■ **Decide when to take questions.** This will probably be at the end. But you might prefer to take questions *during* the presentation. This is more difficult to manage but can improve your relationship with the audience.

■ **Anticipate the most likely questions.** These may be 'Frequently Asked Questions' that you can easily foresee. Others may arise from the particular circumstances of the presentation.

■ **Use a 'plant'.** Ask somebody to be ready with a question to start the session off. Audiences are sometimes hesitant at the end of a presentation about breaking the atmosphere.

■ **Answer concisely.** Force yourself to be brief.

■ **Answer honestly.** You can withhold information, but don't lie. Someone in the audience will almost certainly see through you.

■ **Take questions from the whole audience.** From all parts of the room and from different 'social areas'.

■ **Answer the whole audience.** Don't let questions seduce you into private conversations. Make sure the audience has heard the question.

■ **If you don't know, say so.** And promise what you'll do to answer later.

a simple format for answering a question

■ Repeat the question if necessary. This helps you understand it, helps the audience to hear it, and gives you time to think about your answer.

■ Give a single answer. Make only one point.

■ Now give one reason for your answer.

■ Give an example that illustrates the point.

Of course, it may not be easy to think of all these as you spontaneously respond to a question. But if you slow down and try to think this simple format through, you will probably answer more succinctly and clearly.

putting it in writing

Writing seems to be taking over as a primary means of communication. Many managers now have their own computers and have lost secretarial support. Many secretaries are themselves taking on wider responsibilities, writing their own documents rather than merely typing others'. New working relationships and project management generate more paperwork. And information technology is still largely a medium that demands *text*.

Writing well is probably the most technically difficult form of communication. It requires skill and understanding and a good deal of creativity. And you are judged on the quality of your writing. Writing has to act as your ambassador in your absence. Documents are permanent and can return to haunt you. The worst of it is that there is never one single correct version of any letter or document. You can never check any document for absolute correctness.

Everyone knows effective writing when they see it. It does its job clearly and quickly. It says what the writer wants to say; nothing gets in the way. Above all, effective writing gets results.

writing for results

Whenever you write a business document, you are seeking a result. That's why I prefer the term 'functional writing' to 'business writing'. Functional writing has a job to do. It has a practical purpose.

You don't need to achieve that purpose by writing, of course. Writing is slow and expensive; even writing an e-mail can take time. A telephone call may do the job more quickly. Writing is useful when:

■ you want a permanent record;
■ the information is complicated;
■ you want to copy the same material to many readers.

It may be useful to write to someone who is never available to talk to, though there is no guarantee that they will read your message among the dozens or hundreds they receive that day. Writing also carries a certain authority that conversation may lack. A letter may get action more easily than a phone call because it looks more serious or official.

making reading easier

Most of the advantages of conversation disappear when you write. Compared to talking and listening, writing and reading are slow and inefficient. A document isn't dynamic; it's static. Your reader can't ask it a question because it can't reply. Misunderstandings can easily arise. If the reader gets something wrong, you aren't there to help out.

Good writers try to make reading as easy as possible. Reading, after all, is hard work. People read on three levels, namely:

■ working out what the writer has to say;

- ▓ scanning sentences for complete ideas;
- ▓ reading individual words for their meaning.

To make reading easier, you must help the reader on all three levels. The three golden rules of writing are:

- ▓ use words that the reader is most likely to understand;
- ▓ construct straightforward sentences;
- ▓ make your point, then support it.

Generally, short words are easier to understand than long ones. But your reader will understand best the words that are *familiar* to them. If they know the jargon or the long, abstract words, use them. If in doubt, prefer short words.

Similarly, short sentences are clearer than long ones. But a page full of short sentences will have a 'scatter-gun' effect: lots of points but no connections. Sentences also work best when they are well constructed and grouped together in paragraphs.

The final golden rule is the most important. Most people write in a kind of 'stream of consciousness', putting one idea after another until reaching the conclusion. This gives writing flow. But it is important also to be distinct, making sure that ideas leap out at the reader and hook their attention. If you have something to say, always aim to say it as soon as possible. Then deliver the evidence that supports your idea.

writing step by step

Writing is a task best tackled systematically. The temptation is to do everything at once: working out what to say, in what order, and how to say it. This is a recipe for disaster: you get confused and frustrated and the writing that emerges is a garbled mess. Like cooking, writing is best done step by step.

Think in terms of constructing a document rather than merely writing it. This letter or document has a job to do; you must design and build it to do the job. The construction process has three steps:

- designing the document;
- writing a first draft;
- editing the draft.

Try to keep the stages separate. If you can take breaks between them, so much the better. It can also be useful to ask a colleague for help at each stage.

This chapter looks at these three stages and explores the key issues in each. Many of the techniques will already be familiar to you. The idea of delivering a single message, SPQR and the pyramid structure for organising information all find a place in writing well.

designing the document

We can break planning a document into five stages:

- goal orientation;
- readership analysis;
- creating a message;
- organising information;
- constructing an outline.

goal orientation

Start by identifying the *purpose* of your document. Distinguish between the document's purpose and its subject. Whatever you are writing about, you must be clear what you want to achieve.

Make your purpose as specific as possible. Take care not to create a purpose that is inappropriate. For example, documents cannot analyse or evaluate. These are thinking *processes*. The document will display the *product* of your thinking. It can't do the thinking!

What do you want the document to do? Try these verbs out for size.

'I want this document to...':

recommend	identify	respond
notify	update	summarise
announce	confirm	describe
clarify	invite	propose
compare	justify	request
explain	argue	suggest
highlight	outline	categorise

What do you want the reader to do as a result of reading the document? Functional documents demand action and deliver information to help achieve it. Identify the action you want the reader to take and you will be better placed to provide the information that will help them take it.

What do you want the reader to do? Here are some suggestions.

'I want the reader to...':

target areas for action	realign strategy
attend a meeting	approve funding
implement plan	answer questions
provide input	complete a task
agree with me	review my proposal
choose from options	give me feedback
put something right	investigate an issue

Formalise your objective into a *function statement*. If necessary, agree this with the document's 'client': the person who has asked for it. By agreeing the document's function, you will know exactly what is required of you.

---

function statement

I want this document to
(immediate aim)
so that
(proposed action)

---

readership analysis

Your document may circulate to a wide readership. Different readers will have different expectations, priorities and levels of knowledge. Analyse the readership so that you can organise information in the document most effectively.

managing readership expectations
Categorise your readership into *primary*, *secondary* and *tertiary* readers. The *primary readership* must read the document. The document is designed for them. The *secondary readership* may look at only part of the document. This category may include your manager, who may need to authorise the document before circulation but who will not act on it. The *tertiary readership* may include people you will never meet but who may use the document in some unforeseen way. You will need to satisfy all of these readers. But you must *design* the document for the primary readership alone.

identifying the key persuasive factors
The key persuasive factors are the most important elements in

---

managing readers' expectations

Focus on your primary readership and consider these areas of expectation from their point of view.

Type of document
How does the reader like their documents delivered? Would a presentation be better?
Nature of outcome
Will the reader expect to be given a course of action, or options to consider?
Subject limits
Overview or one part only? Industry practice or internal activities? Departmental or company-wide?
Level of detail
Summary or intimate detail? The same level of detail throughout?
Previous related decisions
What have they done in the past about this or similar issues? What were the results?
Key issues
Where do the reader's priorities lie?
Politics
Who was responsible for creating what you propose to change? Who are the key decision-makers? Who will be affected by change? What are the implications of your proposal?
Wider strategic objectives
How does this material fit with the reader's broad objectives and goals?

---

your reader's decision to believe you. They may arise from the reader's:

- background;
- priorities;
- needs or concerns;
- place in the corporate culture;
- relationship to the external environment.

Put yourself in the primary reader's position and ask: 'What would most convince me about this idea?'.

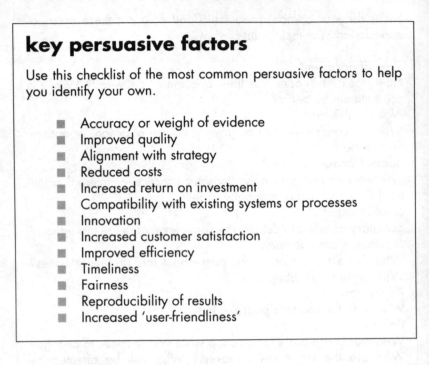

key persuasive factors

Use this checklist of the most common persuasive factors to help you identify your own.

- ■ Accuracy or weight of evidence
- ■ Improved quality
- ■ Alignment with strategy
- ■ Reduced costs
- ■ Increased return on investment
- ■ Compatibility with existing systems or processes
- ■ Innovation
- ■ Increased customer satisfaction
- ■ Improved efficiency
- ■ Timeliness
- ■ Fairness
- ■ Reproducibility of results
- ■ Increased 'user-friendliness'

creating a message

Your document must deliver a single message. The message is the most important element of the document. Everything else in it – the material, how it is ordered, how you present it – depends on the message.

The message is the single most important point you want to make to the reader to express your objective. It is *not* a heading or title. Neither is it a description of what you are doing in the document. The message *expresses* your purpose. Look back at Chapter 5 to find out more about messages. Here is the checklist once again, just to remind you what it should look like. Your document's message should be:

- a sentence;
- expressing a single idea;
- no longer than 15 words long; and
- action-centred.

It is critically important to check that your document's message is appropriate: to you, to the reader, and to your material. In a conversation, interview or presentation, you can check that you are addressing the other person's needs, or the audience's expectations, on the spot. When you write, that interaction disappears. So many documents simply fail to give their readers what they want. SPQR is the only way you can check that you are producing the document that the reader will find useful.

Look back at Chapter 5 for more details about SPQR. Here is a brief summary of the technique, to remind you.

validating the message: SPQR

Construct a story about how the need for the document arose.

Situation
'Once upon a time...' What is the first thing you can say about the matter that you and your reader will agree is true? The starting point is completely uncontroversial.

Problem
What happened to alter the situation? Perhaps something went wrong. Maybe improvements are necessary. Often the problem is that the reader is ignorant of something.

Question
What question does the problem trigger in the reader's mind?

Response
The answer to that question should be the same as your message.

SPQR can:

- help you validate your message;
- facilitate a conversation between writer and reader to clarify the document's message;
- form the core of an Introduction in the document.

organising information

In writing, more than anywhere else, communicating well is a matter of displaying the shape of your thinking. That shape is made up of ideas: the sentences you write. You must arrange those ideas into a coherent shape that the reader can see clearly.

Your reader can understand only one piece of information clearly at a time. To understand your message in more detail, they must first break it into pieces, then understand each piece in order. You must organise information, therefore, in two dimensions:

- vertically (breaking the message into pieces, grouping smaller pieces within larger ones);
- horizontally (organising each group of pieces into an order).

Organising information like this creates a shape that allows the reader's mind to understand complexity in the most natural way. The shape you create is a *pyramid*.

first-stage and second-stage thinking

You can imagine the process of creating the document's structure as a thinking process in two stages. We have already looked at the two stages of thinking as a way of structuring conversations in Chapter 3. Now you can use them to help you organise material for a document:

- *first-stage thinking* – gathering information;
- *second-stage thinking* – organising the information.

Use mindmaps to help you gather information, and the pyramid principle to help you organise it into a coherent structure.

mindmaps

Mindmaps are powerful first-stage thinking tools. By emphasising the links between ideas, they encourage us to think more creatively and efficiently.

To make a mindmap:

- Put a visual image of your subject in the centre of a plain piece of paper.
- Write down anything that comes to mind that connects to the central idea.
- Write single words, in BLOCK CAPITALS, along lines radiating from the centre.
- Main ideas will tend to gravitate to the centre of the map; details will radiate towards the edge.
- Every line must connect to at least one other line.
- Use visual display – colour, pattern, highlights.
- Identify the groups of ideas that you have created. *You should have no more than about six.* Give each a heading and put them into numerical order.

summarising and grouping

Imagine speaking your message to the reader. What question will it provoke in the reader's mind? The question should be one of three:

- 'Why?'
- 'How?'
- 'Which ones?'

You must have at least two answers to the question. Try to

have no more than about six. Write your answers to that question as key points. All your key points must be sentences. You should be able to align each key point with a group of ideas on your mindmap.

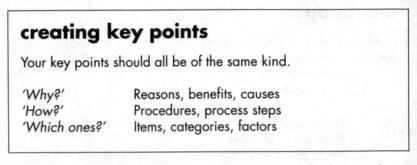

For each key point, ask what question it provokes: 'Why?', 'How?' or 'Which ones?'. Identify the answers to that question and write these as *sub-points*. Repeat if necessary for each sub-point to create *minor points*. For every question, you *must* have more than one answer.

building the pyramid
The result of this question-and-answer process is a pyramid structure.

To summarise, the essential principles of building pyramids are as follows:

- every idea must be a sentence;
- each idea must summarise the ideas grouped beneath it;
- each idea within a group is an answer to the question provoked by the summarising idea.

managing detail
Building a pyramid creates a discipline that allows you to work out how much information to include in your document and how to order it.

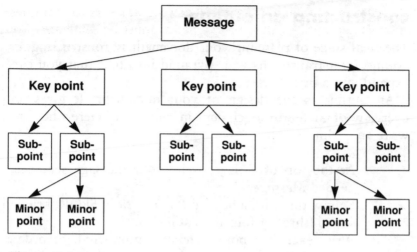

Figure 8.1

Pyramid building always proceeds by division. Each idea provokes a question to which you must have at least two answers – and preferably not more than six. This process of division by question-and-answer continues until an idea fails to provoke a question with multiple answers. It can stop if:

■ an idea does not provoke a question from the reader;
■ an idea provokes a question that has only one answer.

It should never be necessary to create a pyramid containing more than four levels: message, key point, sub-point, minor point.

You must decide how to order ideas in each group. You can order ideas in terms of:

■ rank (size, importance, priority, relevance);
■ process steps;
■ chronology;
■ logical reasoning.

Remember that sometimes the order of ideas is not critical.

constructing an outline

The final stage of planning your document is constructing an outline. This transforms your pyramid into text that you can expand into a first draft.

An outline is the design of your document. It gives an overview of the entire document in miniature. Here's how to write an outline:

- At the top of a page, write your message sentence, headed *Message*.
- Follow this with a headed *Introduction*: SPQR, briefly stated (three or four lines at most).
- Write each key point sentence, numbered, in order, with each sub-point and minor point numbered beneath each key point. Use a decimal numbering system for maximum clarity:
  - 1
  - 1.1
  - 1.1.1 and so on.
- Add a title for the whole outline, and headings for each key point, if necessary.

Once you understand this principle of creating an outline, you can adapt it to any kind of document. Three basic formats will be looked at below: e-mail or memo, letter and report. You'll see that the pyramid remains the same in each case, with only slight variations.

outlining an e-mail or memo

This is the simplest kind of pyramid. Simply place your message at the top, immediately after your salutation. Create a short paragraph – or even a simple bullet point – for each key point and end, if necessary, with a call to action: the next step you want the reader to take.

It's an excellent idea to compress your message into the

subject line of the e-mail so that it appears on the reader's in-box menu.

E-mail is fast becoming a standard mode of communicating in organisations. It's fast, cheap and easy to use. But in many organisations, e-mail is rapidly becoming a problem rather than a solution. Four factors seem to be contributing to this impending crisis:

- **Information overload.** A recent survey suggested that managers receive an average of 178 e-mails a day. Getting yours noticed may be the biggest problem in getting it read.
- **Death of conversation.** Many people now hardly talk to each other; they send e-mails instead. As a result, e-mail is becoming infected with substitutes for social contact. Lonely cubicle workers spread gossip in private jargon, spiced with cryptic symbols.
- **More haste, less understanding.** The style of writing in e-mail is becoming relaxed to the point of being garbled.
- **Overflowing in-boxes.** When was the last time you weeded your in-box?

E-mail *is* writing. Treat it as you would any other kind of writing: plan; write; edit. Here are 10 more tips to help e-mail work better for you:

- Make your message clear.
- Minimise information. Don't make the reader scroll down.
- Put the message in the subject line. It's much more useful to have a headline-style message in this line than a heading.
- Don't shout. Avoid capital letters, underlining and bold. Above all, avoid facetious or all-purpose headings such as 'Urgent' or 'Read this now!'.

- Don't fan 'flames'. Don't write anything in an e-mail that you wouldn't say face-to-face.
- Avoid emoticons. Don't use symbols or silly abbreviations. Use English.
- Edit before sending. E-mail is so fast that you can easily spend a few moments checking sense, spelling and punctuation.
- Remember that e-mail is public. Most e-mail can be accessed on central servers. Never write anything that a lawyer might use against you.
- Don't spam. Send only messages that you must send, to the individuals who need to read them. Avoid blanket copies. (Spam is junk e-mail.)
- Clear your in-box regularly. You'll make the system – and yourself – work much more efficiently.

outline of an e-mail

Re: conference meeting, 2 April: key issues
Derek
There are three key issues I'd like to discuss at our meeting on Friday.

- How can we promote the conference more effectively abroad?
- How can we align the main speakers' messages effectively to support corporate strategy?
- Do we have the resources to create an informal exhibition area in the foyer?

If you have any other issues to raise, copy me in. See you there!
Gloria

outlining a letter

The pyramid here is framed by handshakes: one at the start, and possibly one at the end. The style of a letter may differ slightly from that of an e-mail (there will be more on style later), but apart from that, and a few other formalities of layout, the two are similar.

---

outline of a letter

25 January 2000   *[company logo]*
Sidney Reader
Readership House
READERTOWN
AB1 2CD

Dear Sidney
Thank you for your letter of 20 January.   *[handshake]*
This is my main message.   *[message sentence]*
My first point is here.   *[paragraphs]*
...
My second point is here.
...
The next step is...   *[action point]*
I hope this is satisfactory.   *[closing handshake]*

Yours sincerely
Alan Writer
Job title

---

outlining a report

Reports tend to need the fullest kind of outline, complete with summary, introduction, numbered points and an array of sub-points and minor points. Creating the outline is a really useful stage in constructing a report. You can use the outline to check with the report's 'client' that it is developing as they would wish, to make changes to your report without having to rewrite lots of text, and to establish that you know exactly what your key ideas are for each section. The outline can itself form the summary of the report. It will also be invaluable for those readers who only want reports that cover a single sheet of A4. For them, the outline *is* the report.

---

outline of a report

Message
We should locate new plant in Gatheringham.

Introduction
Our business is rapidly expanding. Existing manufacturing plant will reach capacity within three years. We urgently need to decide where to locate new manufacturing plant. This document summarises the findings of the relocation project and justifies its recommendation in strategic terms.

1. Capital costs in Gatheringham are estimated at 10% below those of the next best location.
    1.1 Constructors' bids in the area average 10% below those in other locations.
    1.2 Land costs are on average 13% lower than in other areas.
2. Operating costs in Gatheringham are estimated to be 15% lower than in other areas.
    2.1 Labour costs are 7% less than the national average.
    2.2 Overheads are estimated at 9% less than in current plants.
    2.3 Tax incentives for operating in this zone are very attractive.
3. Distribution costs would decrease by at least 7% if centred on Gatheringham.
    3.1 The area is centrally located for our markets.
    3.2 The local infrastructure is well developed.

---

writing a first draft

Writing the document should be considerably easier now that the outline is complete. Essentially, you need to expand the outline by adding text, headings, and – for reports in particular – numbering and graphics. The plan of the outline is in place, and the sentences in the outline give you a clear idea of what you want to say in each paragraph and section.

Think of writing the first draft of your document as a separate activity from either planning or editing. Be guided by the following principles:

■ **Write quickly.** Don't ponder over words. Keep going. Leave gaps if necessary. Aim for a natural flow.

■ **Write in your own voice.** Expressing yourself in your own way will help you to say what you mean more exactly. If your reader can 'hear' your voice, reading will be easier.

■ **Write without interruption.** Try to find a time and place where you can think and write without distractions.

■ **Write without editing.** Don't try to get it right first time. Resist the temptation to edit as you go. You will tend to get stuck and waste time.

■ **Keep to the plan of your outline.** Use the sentences from your outline to focus what you want to say. If you find yourself wandering from the point, stop and move on to the next sentence in the outline.

navigation aids

Effective documents contain navigation aids to help the reader find their way around. The most important of these are:

■ summaries;

■ introductions;
■ headings;
■ bullet points.

All of these elements will help you 'sell' the document to your reader.

summaries and introductions

Don't confuse these two essential items. The first, the *summary*, is the document in miniature. At its heart is your message. Place the summary at the very start of the document – immediately following the title page. Your outline is a ready-made summary.

The second, the *introduction*, explains how the document came into being. At its heart is SPQR: background information, including the problem addressed by the document and the question it answers. Introductions might expand to include:

■ methodology;
■ acknowledgements;
■ a short guide to the document, section by section.

headings

Pay close attention to the title and other headings in your document. They should have high scanning value: the reader should be able to glean a lot of information from relatively few words. 'Financial review', for example, has low scanning value. 'Breakdown of operating costs 2000' works rather better.

In a report, you might assemble your headings into a contents list. Check it to see that the headings give a fair idea of content and are not too repetitious.

bullet points

Bullet points are visually very powerful. There is a danger, therefore, that you can use them too much. Don't overuse them. Follow these guidelines:

- Construct the points in parallel. All items should be grammatically of the same kind.
- Make the points consistent with the 'platform' – the text that introduces the list.
- Improve the 'platform' so that repeated elements in the list need be expressed only once.

editing the draft

The aim of editing is to make the first draft easier to read.

Editing is about making choices. It is potentially endless because there is never only one way to say what you mean. It's especially difficult to edit your own work. Ask a colleague to help you if you can. Take a break before editing so that you are better prepared to look at the text afresh.

Edit systematically. Editing word by word is time-consuming and may be counterproductive. To edit efficiently, work on three separate levels in the following order:

- paragraphs;
- sentences;
- words.

It's probably best to edit hard copy, rather than on screen.

creating effective paragraphs

Paragraphs display the shape of your thinking. They show the individual main ideas and the relationships between them. Every time you take a step, alter your point of view or change direction, you should start a new paragraph.

Use a *topic sentence* at the start of each paragraph to summarise it. Topic sentences help you to decide what to include in each paragraph. You can think of a topic sentence as the paragraph's message. It should:

- be a fully grammatical sentence;
- make a single point;
- contain no more than about 15 words;
- say something new.

An outline, of course, is a ready source of topic sentences. Another place to look for potential topic sentences is at the end of a paragraph. Very often people put the most important idea as the paragraph's conclusion. Try flipping that conclusion to the start of the paragraph as a topic sentence. Topic sentences should make sense in order. You should be able to read all the topic sentences and understand a section in summary.

editing a paragraph

To minimise potential downtime and operational risk, it is recommended that the business case for the purchase of a back-up server, which could also be used for system testing, be formally examined. We are now addressing this since a decision is needed by the end of March to avoid additional hire costs or the loss of the rented machine.

Note how a topic sentence allows the writer to cut down the paragraph considerably and improve readability.

We are now examining the business case for buying a back-up server. This could:

- *minimise potential down-time;*
- *minimise operational risk;*
- *also be used for system testing.*

A decision is needed by the end of March to avoid extra hire costs or the loss of the rented machine.

sentence construction

Sentences express ideas. They will express your ideas more strongly if they are constructed sturdily. Sentences are weak when they are too long or poorly built. Aim always in your sentences to say what you mean *and no more*.

Follow the '15–25' rule. Message sentences, topic sentences and other sentences expressing big ideas should never exceed 15 words. All other sentences should keep within 25 words.

---

editing a long sentence

It was originally planned that data conversion and implementation across the remaining business areas would follow at the end of September 1996, but following a variety of problems, considerable scope drift, changes of personnel on the project team and several amendments to the timetable, conversion did not take place until 1 April 1997 and some users were still using parts of the old system until it was finally disconnected in July 1997.

This is easily improved by cutting the sentence at the conjunctions – but, and – and using a vertical list.

The project team originally planned to convert data and implement the system in remaining business areas at the end of September 1996. However, conversion was delayed by changes in:

- ■ *the scope of the project;*
- ■ *personnel on the project team;*
- ■ *the timetable.*

The system was finally converted on 1 April 1997. Some users continued to use parts of the old system until it was disconnected in July 1997.

editing words

English has a huge vocabulary. One of the main reasons is that the language is a hybrid, so many ideas can be expressed by two or three words. Maybe for this reason more than any other, plain English has grown up as a way of helping people to choose the best words for their needs.

Plain English helps any reader to understand at first reading. It tells the truth without embellishment. It is a code of practice, not a set of rigid rules.

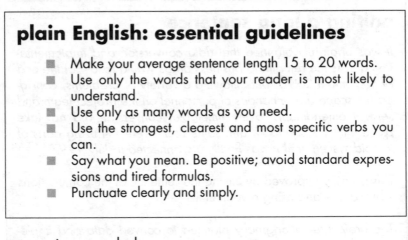

plain English: essential guidelines

- Make your average sentence length 15 to 20 words.
- Use only the words that your reader is most likely to understand.
- Use only as many words as you need.
- Use the strongest, clearest and most specific verbs you can.
- Say what you mean. Be positive; avoid standard expressions and tired formulas.
- Punctuate clearly and simply.

managing vocabulary

Certain words cause particular problems with readability. Pay attention in particular to:

- passive verbs;
- abstract nouns;
- unnecessary words.

passive verbs

Verbs can be either active or passive. An active verb expresses what its subject does; a passive verb expresses what its subject suffers. Sentences with active verbs are shorter, stronger and more dynamic than those with passive ones.

*It is **anticipated** that additional disk space **may be needed**.*

We anticipate that the system will need additional disk space.

abstract nouns

Nouns name things, people, times, places and qualities. *Concrete nouns* name things physically present in the world (table, woman, pen, car, tree); *abstract nouns* name ideas, concepts and qualities that cannot be sensed physically (growth, awareness, training, marketing, possibility).

Try to cut down your use of abstract nouns. Replace them, if you can, with verbs or adjectives. If you can replace an abstract noun only with a group of shorter, more concrete words, consider keeping it.

*There were some **differences** in configuration between the two machines, which added a **degree** of **complexity** to the **exercise**.*

The two machines were configured differently, making the exercise more complex.

unnecessary words

Some words contribute nothing to meaning. You might use them because they sound good, or because you don't know what to say next. Remove them.

The benefits of this arrangement are a saving in consultancy costs and the opportunity for new users to learn the system in a meaningful situation at the same time as they learn their jobs.

This arrangement saves consultancy costs and allows new users to learn the system as part of on-the-job learning.

developing a readable style

Bringing your own writing to life is a long-term project. Here are some guidelines to point you in the right direction:

- Say what you mean.
- Be specific.
- Be positive.
- Remove blockages.

Style is personal. Choosing how to write is like choosing how to dress. Improving your style is not unlike improving your dress sense. Look around; imitate what you admire; aim for functional elegance rather than excessive flamboyance.

say what you mean
Concentrate on what you want to say, not how to say it. Imagine the reader's response. If you only had a few seconds to get your point across, what would you say?

- Write down your key messages as boldly as possible.
- Imagine speaking what you have written. Could you say it more simply?
- Be sincere. Don't wrap your meaning up in fancy language.
- Don't use 'scaffolding'. Avoid describing what you are doing in the document.

be specific
Aim to be precise rather than vague. Avoid generalising.

- Use numbers. Ration them, so that you don't blind the reader with statistics. Avoid words that convey a general sense of number (*several, lots, few*) or that are value-loaded (*excessive, insufficient, unacceptable, gigantic*) – unless you can support the judgement with numbers.
- Write personally. Use names. Allocate responsibility for actions. Use personal pronouns wherever appropriate, but take care not to overuse them.
- Use verbs with a specific meaning. Avoid verbs that

don't mean much (*get, carry out, perform, give, conduct, implement, move, do*). In particular, try to find crisper alternatives to the verbs *to have* and *to be*.
▓ Make it concrete. Give real examples.
▓ Use jargon carefully. If your reader will understand an idea better in jargon, use it. Very often, however, we use jargon to cover our own *lack* of clear understanding. Don't use jargon as an excuse for not knowing quite what you mean.

be positive
The best functional writing is forward-looking and action-centred. Avoid writing too much about what has happened, what hasn't happened, what should have happened or what's wrong.

▓ Write about proposals, future action, how to put things right, what you are doing.
▓ Make definite promises.
▓ Generate in your reader the feeling appropriate to the message. Avoid emotive language.

remove blockages
Good writing flows like water in a pipe. The words should be under pressure. Remove blockages so that the meaning flows freely.

▓ Transform passive verbs into active ones.
▓ Replace abstract nouns with concrete ones.
▓ Remove unnecessary words or groups of words.
▓ Exterminate clichés.
▓ Puncture inflated language. You can easily tell if a word is inflated. If you remove it, would you need a group of words to say the same thing? If so, the word is not inflated. If not, find a shorter alternative or remove the word completely.

■ Make sure your sentences connect clearly. Vary your sentence construction: a short sentence at the start of a paragraph; longer, more complex sentences to develop a theme.

appendix: where to go from here

Communication is continuous, and we never finish learning how to improve. Here are some thoughts about books that will take further the ideas that have been explored in this book.

chapter 1: what is communication?

Steven Mithen's (1998) book, *The Prehistory of the Mind* (Phoenix, London) discusses the origins of communication in primate activity. Margaret Wheatley's (1992) *Leadership and the New Science* (Berret-Koehler, San Fransisco) brings insights from quantum theory and complexity to bear on ideas of information.

chapter 2: how conversations work

William Isaac's (1999) *Dialogue and the Art of Thinking Together* (Currency Books, New York) is at the leading edge of studies of conversation.

chapter 3: seven ways to improve your conversations

First- and second-stage thinking are notions that inform Edward de Bono's work. Look at *Lateral Thinking in Management* (Penguin, London, 1982). The four types of conversation derive from the work of Michael Wallacek.

Chris Argyris' Ladder of Inference is best found in *The Fifth Discipline Fieldbook*, edited by Peter Senge and others (Nicholas Brealey, London, 1994).

For more on mindmaps, see Tony Buzan's (1974) *Use your Head* (BBC, London).

chapter 4: the skills of enquiry

Nancy Kline's (1999) *Time to Think* (Ward Lock, London) is a fascinating new-look study of deep listening.

chapter 5: the skills of persuasion

Peter Thompson's (1999) *Persuading Aristotle* (Kogan Page, London) entertainingly relates classical rhetoric to modern business techniques. For more on pyramids, look at Barbara Minto's (1987) *The Pyramid Principle* (Pitman, London).

chapter 6: interviews

Alan Barker's (2000) *How to be Better at Managing people* (Kogan Page, London) discusses all of these types of interview, and other kinds of managerial conversation, in more depth.

For more on coaching, John Whitmore's (1992) *Coaching for Performance* (Nicholas Brealey, London) is a central text. Reg Hamilton's (1993) *Mentoring* (Industrial Society, London) contains some useful material on counselling.

chapter 7: making a presentation

Look at *How to be Better at Giving Presentations* by Michael Stevens (Kogan Page, London, 1996) for further advice. Peter Thompson's (1999) *Persuading Aristotle* (Kogan Page, London) also includes a chapter on presenting.

chapter 8: putting it in writing

Alan Barker's (1999) *Writing at Work* (Industrial Society, London) is a comprehensive guide to writing business documents.